Editors for the Tim Stüttgen Archiv: Max Jorge Hinderer, Liad Kantorowicz, Nicolas Siepen, Margarita Tsomou
www.timstuettgen.org
Lectorate and Editing: Daniel Hendrickson, Max Jorge Hinderer, Margarita Tsomou
Assistance during the writing process: Katya Sander and Carsten Juhl
Layout: Nicolas Siepen
Special thanks to Martina Petrelli and Kim Feser for the layout support
Proofreading: Hypatia Vourloumi and Teodora Tabacki

Cover: Poem by Tim Stüttgen, written for *Drama per Musica*, a dance-performance by Alexandre Roccoli
Cover photography by Lee Santa: *Sun Ra Arkestra* (1968)
www.lee-santa.artistwebsites.com

Printed by agit-druck GmbH, Berlin, Germany
Published by b_books BERLIN
b_books, Lübbener Str. 14, 10997 Berlin, Germany
www.bbooks.de / verlag@bbooks.de
copyright 2014

Co-published with autonomedia NEW YORK
Autonomedia, POB 568, Brooklyn, NY 11211-0568 USA
www.autonomedia.org / info@autonomedia.org

Special issue of SUM magazine
ISBN 978-3-942214-16-2

Distribution: b_books, autonomedia, anagram, Kunstakademiet ToF
www.bbooks.de / www.autonomedia.org / www.anagrambooks.com / carsten.juhl@kunstakademiet.dk

In a Qu*A*re Time and Place

Post-Slavery Temporalities, Blaxploitation, and Sun Ra's Afrofuturism
between Intersectionality and Heterogeneity

Tim Stüttgen

*

Edited by the Tim Stüttgen Archiv

b_books

*

Co-published with autonomedia NY

This is a special issue of SUM magazine, published by b_books, Berlin, in accordance with the publishing house of The Royal Danish Academy of Fine Arts, Schools of Visual Art, Copenhagen.

To Timi

In a Qu*A*re Time and Place

By Tim Stüttgen

Table of Contents

1.0   Intro / 8
1.1   On the Use of Categories and Concepts / 17
1.2   Chapter Overview / 18

2.0   Slavery as Epistemological Break in Gender and Queer Studies / 23
2.1   Fanon and the Black Experience / 28
2.2   Fanon in the Cinema, Waiting / 34
2.3   The Black Danger and the White Nation / 35
2.4   The Sexualization of Racism / 42

3.0   Black Films with Blacks with Guns / 48
3.1   A Minoritarian Cinema: The Black Movement-Image / 54
3.2   Reading Blaxploitation, Intersectionally / 61

4.0   QuAre Theory and the Heterogeneity of Black Situativity / 76
4.1   Homonationalism and Biopolitics / 81
4.2   Queer Times / 89

5.0   Introducing: Sun Ra / 94
5.1   Sun Ra and the Question of Homosexuality / 100
5.2   Afrofuturism: Genealogical Notes / 103
5.3   From the Slave to the Alien, from the Slaveship to the Spaceship / 105
5.4   Beyond Black Nationalism: The Black Atlantic / 116

6.0   Space Is the Place: The Black Time-Image / 121
6.1   The Subversion of the Black Entertainer / 128
6.2   Duel with the Overseer: Challenging the Black Macho / 132
6.3   QuAring the Community: Beyond Black Authenticity / 138
6.4   Dixie Music: Bound to the Past? / 146
6.5   The Present Is Not Enough: Futures of the QuAre Performative / 149

7.0   The Arkestra: Sonic Ecstasy / 152
7.1   Collective Improvisation / 155
7.2   QuAre Assemblage Production / 159

8.0   Outro / 165
9.0   Bibliography * Links of Imagery * Films / 170
      Post-Scriptum: Editors' notes by Katya Sander, Margarita Tsomou and Daniel Hendrickson / 182

1.0 Intro

*

Maybe I should start with a personal anecdote. Back in the day, among many other newspapers and magazines, I was writing for Germany's biggest hip-hop magazine, *Juice*. Even if there was nothing radically political about the magazine, it gave me the chance to interview and meet some of the central figures of rap culture. Very often, my whiteness would raise suspicion, and only through our conversation, when the MCs and producers would find out that I had a lot of respect and knowledge about their issues, both musical and political, would an intimate dialogue open up. This gave me the privilege of hearing *black* oral history first hand. Hip-hop is a complex and creative culture that I learned to love after seeing the art of breakdance in films like *Wild Style* (Charlie Ahearn, 1983) and *Beat Street* (Stan Lathan, 1984) and the creativity of the graffiti on the walls of my small hometown in western Germany. And of course I loved rap, which was introduced to me by fellow skater friends, or by the first *German* rap groups, mostly consisting of migrants (like Fresh Familee or Advanced Chemistry) in youth centers I would visit, not to mention the legendary TV show *Yo! MTV Raps*, which I was able to watch after my parents got cable television. Thus I experienced the emergence of the fruitful interrelation between American rap culture and a new scene of *Germans* and migrants in Europe who were creating a worldwide interface to express (and teach me about) exclusion, classism and *racism*. As Fatima El-Tayeb argues, hip-hop culture is arguably Europe's "most important transborder counterpublic site,"[1] a site that also took elements from the US to express its own, postnational perspective on the politics of belonging and against new forms of racism:

---

[1] Fatima El-Tayeb, *European Others – Queering Ethnicity in Postnational Europe* (Minneapolis: University of Minnesota Press, 2011) xl.

*

> The tide of racist violence that swept Europe in the early 1990s politicized many young people of color who could not relate to the politics of traditional migrant and antiracist groups. Hip-hop culture created a framework in which European ethnic "(un)subjects" for the first time were able to create a language through which they could express their specific experiences, define themselves as autonomous, and position themselves in relation to the struggles of American communities of color...[2]

Hip-hop culture was one of the first minor subcultures that connected affirmation and politics, partying and a discourse against migrant exclusion – and I was proud and grateful to have it in my life. It made me learn a lot about racism and non-western codes of belonging, and it gave me shelter when I felt lonely as I moved to live in a bigger, more urban city like London. I wrote many articles for *Juice* and met Afrocentric-conscious MCs like Talib Kweli, new rhyme innovators like Dizzee Rascal or Aesop Rock and multicultural rap traditionalists like the Dilated Peoples and great female soul divas like Truth Hurts.[3] But sooner or later I reached a limit.

Because of my then somewhat confused bisexuality and interest in crossdressing (next to obvious privileges as a white, middle-class boy with German citizenship), I never felt like I really belonged in a movement that seemed very dominated by sexism and homophobia. When I heard about homo-hop and other queer articulations in rap, such as the Deep Dick Collective or Jen-Ro, it seemed that I could

---

[2] El-Tayeb 30.
[3] At this time, my work obviously wasn't limited to hip-hop. It also included jazz, trip-hop, reggae, dub and German leftist underground discourse rock. It opened the world to a whole oral history of black music and culture to me.

*

connect what I learned from a matriarchal, feminist family structure with the impulses of the hip-hop world. Finally I proposed to *Juice* that I write a big report on queer rap artists — something that had never happened before in this scope in the history of German music journalism. They accepted, but still acted a little bit paranoid, possibly worried about homophobic reactions from their mostly young, male and straight readership. Even though the story was one of the biggest in the issue, they wouldn't note its existence on their cover. What was also odd was that they wouldn't put any photo of the featured artists (Juba Kalamka and DDC, Deadlee, Jen-Ro, Godess and She) in the article, which gave the story a somewhat strange dimension, as the queer rappers seemed to have no actual bodies and faces. Maybe I'm exaggerating — but the real strange thing happened after that. As if through an unspoken contract, this was the last article I ever wrote for *Juice* magazine. I was never again asked to submit a story or review an album. And I never asked them again either, and alternatively got caught up in the inspiring and emerging queer world just becoming a trademark for affirmative politics and deviant subcultural production and lifeforms in Europe — and especially in Berlin.

I had certainly known gay culture and cabaret from a young age, since my uncle was supposedly gay — and I became inspired by phenomena such as the drag king community in Cologne and the books on queer theory by icons like Judith Butler, Judith "Jack" Halberstam, Eve Kosovsky Sedgwick, and Beatriz "Beto" Preciado. Soon, inspired by my then-partner who became interested in transgender politics, I would start doing *drag* myself and luckily I got a scholarship to work on a subject that gave me a certain visibility in the queer academic world: *postpornography*. Obviously, a lot of amazing work has been

*

done in gender and queer studies regarding the visual. Becoming an outspoken supporter of queer politics and theories myself, most notably through my work on queer feminist interventions in porn,[4] but also through my journalism and my drag performances, I argued for a radicalization of sexual politics and with it, the universalization of its ideals. But again, only concentrating on one or two categories of power, in this sense gender and sexuality, made other dynamics and forms of exclusion merely invisible. I remember, for instance, how I was invited, along with many other fellow queer activists and performers from Europe, the US, and Canada, to take part in the performative wedding of the LoveArtLab in 2009, Annie Sprinkle's and her partner Elizabeth Stephen's project about postporn love and queering marriage. This glamorous event at the Biennale in Venice was really a blast and created one of the highlights of my postporn life. It made me aware of how stimulating and successful queer visual politics have been as interventions and new forms of community building beyond a still very male-dominated and heteronormative art world. While white queer artists like Andy Warhol, Jack Smith, or Annie Sprinkle and Catherine Opie have become partly incorporated into the art canon, queer-of-color positions have mostly remained invisible or at least secondary and marginal. Therefore, again, I reached a limit. While my interest in rap, next to soul and jazz music, seemed mostly to happen in a heteronormative world, my interest in queer feminist cultures and theories seemed mostly unmarked white. Also, emerging discussions about queer-of-color politics and emerging critical whiteness studies proved to me that there was no political space in Germany that was naturally given to the ones who suffer from double discrimination and multiple forms of exclusion. The phenomenon of

---

4 See Tim Stüttgen, ed., *Post/Porn/Politics* (Berlin: b_books, 2010)

*

pornography seemed indirectly to prolong a very western discourse of sexual freedom while unintentionally ignoring the queer feminist issues of black sexworkers[5] or Arab women. Of course my intention is not to blame Annie and Beth or the emerging queer porn world for the invisibility of queers of color in their project. But sooner or later I became aware of how embedded the notion of queer feminist pornography is in a predominately western white narrative of sexual liberation. This narrative would not only clash with persons of color in queer subcultures and the sex industry, as their experiences of racism have mostly been overlooked, but also with a new phase of imperial discourses and wars that have been taking place since 9/11. Obviously, things seem to have shifted in recent years. While some queers were associated with illness and death by a homophobic culture during the early days of the AIDS crisis, now they are interpellated as good citizens, consumers, or even patriots and soldiers. As Jasbir Puar notes, while some communities became targeted for life, others became "targeted for death."[6]

At the same time, just to name one obvious example, communities that were marked as colored would become the new outsiders that symbolize backwardness and regression[7].

---

[5] Just think of how the BDSM figure of the slave might seem different for somebody who stems him or herself from a black tradition that experienced real slavery and its aftermath. This doesn't mean though, that there are no non-western artists changing pornographic representation, including interactions with BDSM practices. To name just a few, there are Dumb Type from Japan, Shu Lea-Cheang from Taiwan, Afro-British video artist Isaac Julien, or Indian postporn filmmaker Tejal Shah.
[6] Jasbir Puar, *Terrorist Assemblages: Homonationalism in Queer Times* (Durham: Duke University Press, 2007) 36.
[7] This is obviously not an argument against the inclusion of some queers into more liveable lives, but a reflection on a situation where the inclusion of some goes along with the exclusion of others.

*

In this book I am not trying to universally and finally represent or solve contemporary discussions about gender, sexuality, race, class, nation, and ethnicity. But by concentrating on a very central and traumatic historical event — slavery — and the emancipatory struggles of Afro-Americans, we can see how patterns of racist discourses work to address the supposedly dangerous and backwards colored body. At that time, it was the *dangerous* and always presumably *homophobic* black man who had to be domesticated, caught and brought to prison; now these same logics are encountered by, for instance, the *dangerous* Arabs,[8] and new forms of emerging racism and Islamophobia are executed through new policies in European countries — partly using feminist and queer arguments to perform exclusion in a progressive costume.[9] Furthermore slavery makes us aware of a central contradiction of the Enlightenment project. While universal freedom for everybody was the core of the Enlightenment message, the same people who were proclaiming universal freedom were the ones installing slavery and colonialism in other countries. The biggest kidnapping of history intersected with brutal forms of torture, forced labor, and exploitation next to the dehumanization of potentially any non-white or non-western subject. It is no wonder that in these conditions the relations of, for instance, gender and race have to be thought of and understood differently than those of their white contemporaries. As non-white bodies have been the objects of

---

8 Even if there are obvious similarities between racisms against blacks and Arabs, it doesn't mean that this book provides a metaphor. It specifically deals with post-slavery in the Afro-American context and cannot be translated easily into other times and places. While Eurocentric arguments are very central in contemporary forms of racism, this research is clearly limited to the history of slavery and black liberation in the USA.

9 This contemporary problem is addressed, for example, in queer-of-color interventions. See Puar, *Terrorist Assemblages* for the American and El-Tayeb, *European Others* for the European context.

*

forms of racism that clearly sexualized them, their sexuality, or even their queerness, appears in different ways. Concentrating on black articulations of the post-slavery age, a time when concrete slavery was abolished but the regressive core of its discourses survived in texts, images, and minds, I hope to shed light on an alternative narrative of black sexualities, one that I will later try to define, inspired by E. Patrick Johnson, as quAre.

Thus, the central question of this work is how different methodological approaches — the anti-categorial notion of queer theory and the multi-categorial perspective of intersectionality — can come into dialogue for the proposition of a quAre theory. QuAre takes the "A" of the black and puts it in the middle of queer. One special ingredient in this work is the philosophy of Gilles Deleuze. While Deleuze has long been criticized by gender and queer theorists, it is worth noting that these days queer-of-color theorists like Kara Keeling and Jasbir Puar have started a new dialogue with the philosopher. Deleuze's theory is not only extra-ordinary when he tries to think identity beyond structural categories like gender, sexuality, or race but proposes a more complex model of heterogeneity that goes beyond dualisms and identity labels. This heterogeneity seems to become more and more important for queer scholars to first, think beyond dualisms and categories but second, to grasp the complexity of queer of color subjects, who always seemed to have to choose between, for instance, the stereotypical antagonisms of a supposedly white queer-feminist movement and a supposedly black heteronormative movement. Therefore this work tries to deepen a dialogue between Deleuzian and queer-of-color approaches, arguing for a position that is mindful of both intersectional approaches that address multiple

*

categories of power, and of anti-categorial approaches that try to get beyond notions of categoriality, without merely choosing the one or the other. Instead, this study tries to show how they productively resonate with each other. Furthermore, Deleuze constructed a very unique film theory, which deals with the two major categories that come into play in this text: movement and time. In this sense I follow Kara Keeling when she writes: "I argue that 'the black image' and 'the white image' are inherently problematic and that the black image might be best understood in terms of the spatiotemporal relations it makes visible."[10]

Movement and time are central formal and philosophical categories when dealing with the cultural material I am looking at. Film and music exist in and through them. Also, when dealing with such a heavy issue as post-slavery in the American context, movement is central, since it was concretely taken from the slaves, while time is central, since colonial time seemed endless for its victims. Thus, the desire for another time, where blacks could move freely, was possibly the biggest desire shared by the people who were kidnapped from Africa. But before we look at some visual articulations of the dreams of black movements and times, we start at the nightmare of the black experience in the temporality of colonialism. For we can only grasp the lines of flight and escape routes from slavery if we start to understand how powerful and problematic the duality of whiteness and blackness is as it is experienced by the black man, as Fanon would call it.

---

[10] Kara Keeling, *The Witch's Flight: The Cinematic, the Black Femme, and the Image of Common-Sense* (Durham: Duke University Press, 2007) 27.

*

1.1 On the Use of Categories and Concepts

There are three types of terms that are written in italics* in this work. First and most importantly, the categories of power, such as race,[11] gender, sexuality, class, and so on. First, this relates to the constructedness of the terms. By writing them in italics, I am trying to underline that these terms are ideological terms while being central and relational for the analysis of power relations in this study. Writing them in italics thus refers both to the fact that I understand them not in essentialist, but in constructed terms, while I also want to highlight their political centrality and their relatedness, such as, for instance, in white and black, or queer and quAre. Second, there are concepts that more or less directly relate to the terms, like, for instance, queer futures or Black Atlantic, so here, the relationship between the central categorial terms and the political concepts are highlighted. Thus, by writing both categories and concepts in italics, both their constructedness and their relatedness are underlined.

Third, negative and derogatory terms and concepts, such as the sexualization of racism are also set in italics, as they relate to the same power-dynamics that are put into question in this analysis. This makes, as the reader will see, a lot of italics altogether, but shall also produce a sensibility for the categories of power and relational categories in question and make the reader, in a sense, stumble

---

11 Especially a term like "race" and its German equivalent "Rasse" has a very problematic and destructive history. However, I apply the concept of race stemming from anti-racist discplines like Critical Race Studies, where the term is understood both in its powerful dimension such as in the process of racialization, but also in its anti-essentialist and strategic sense for anti-racist analysis and anti-racist counterpositioning. For further discussion on the problematics of the term "race," see Ina Kerner, *Differenzen der Macht. Zur Anatomie von Rassismus und Sexismus* (Frankfurt am Main: Campus Verlag, 2009) 113-140.

*

again and again over the italics and thereby become sensitive to the relational categories s/he is dealing with.

* After a lengthy discussion among the editors of this publication, the decision was finally made not to follow the author's elaborate use of italicization. The reasons for this are detailed in the editors' note.

1.2 Chapter Overview

Chapter 2 will introduce slavery as one of the basic contradictions of modernity. "Slavery as Epistomological Break in Gender and Queer Studies" addresses the basic contradiction of the Enlightenment project. While some subjects have been included in the notion of the human, others have not — and while freedom was announced for everybody, slaves were basically the complete opposite of free while their labor was exploited in order to found the modern world. Thus, the difference between western and non-western, white and black subjects addresses the point to start from in this study. As Hortense Spillers notes, even the differentiation between male and female was not at all a primary category for the black slaves.[12] Both similarly exploited and used, tortured and killed, the notion of the nuclear family, including the reproductive and private sphere, which was addressed by white feminists, was, for the black captivated subjects/objects, far from reach. Thus, my analysis starts at the difference between black and white bodies in colonial times, which is addressed by Frantz Fanon. Fanon makes a striking outline of the ontology of the black man, whose experience of racism is discussed in "Fanon and the Black Experience." I especially take note of how the blacks'

[12] Hortense Spillers, "Mama's Baby, Papa's Maybe: An American Grammar Book", *Diacritics*, Summer 1987, vol. 17, no. 2 (1997).

*

appearance is experienced through the gaze of whites and how this causes affective and corporeal negativity in the blacks' body. The trauma of colonial time is also at the center in "Fanon in the Cinema, Waiting," where the endless repetition of derogatory images of the black is discussed and addressed through an anecdote of sitting in the cinema and being exposed to white fantasies on the screen. However, the potential of breaking the vicious cycle is addressed through the notion of the *explosive* black, as for Fanon the radical negativity of decolonial violence can break the vicious circle where the black man experiences himself as a toy in the hands of the white man. An analysis of the racist film classic *Birth of a Nation* (D.W. Griffith, 1915) illustrates Fanon's experience of white supremacist fantasies. In the center of the film analysis we see the construction of the black as a *public danger*, a *monster* and a *rapist*, a stereotype that is used to put him back in captivity — just as the slaves once were. The final part of Chapter 2 looks at the sexualization of racism and intersections of sexist and racist science through further examples both male and female.

Chapter 3 returns to the notion of the *explosive* and *phallic* black, to racist images that became appropriated and used for black liberation. First, through the interventions of the Black Panthers as *blacks with guns*. Following Kara Keeling, I argue that at the moment the images of the Black Panthers intervened in the public and in the media, another black future was addressed by breaking the vicious cycle of *colonial time* precisely by representing *blacks with guns* and thereby autonomy from the helplessness in their relation to the police. These images were also central motifs of Blaxploitation cinema, where the *phallic* and *armed* black gives rise to the black movement-image.

*

Deleuze's notion of narrative cinema, which is structured through movement, montage, and identification with the main character, gets a new political nuance through the black in movement that is the central motif of Blaxploitation and with it, a first cinematic attempt to show blacks that succeed in surviving the narrative. A discussion of intersectionality then opens up to a closer look at Blaxploitation. The differentiation of the genre is analyzed through the categories of race, gender, and sexuality from an intersectional perspective. A final perspective also looks at the possibilities of reading Blaxploitation films as queer.

Chapter 4 establishes a deepening discussion about the intersection of queer and critical race studies. Following E. Patrick Johnson, the specific notion of quAre theory is addressed, followed by an investigation of how the experience of blackness in connection to gender and sexuality recognizes different subject positions that are marked as non-reproductive beyond the dualism of heterosexuality and homosexuality that seemed so central in white hegemonic queer studies. A further, more current investigation of how racism is intertwined with nationalism comes through the discussion of *homonationalism* and biopolitics. Biopolitics is a politics that controls and disciplines the human *as a species* and differentiates between humans that are included into the reproduction of the *nation* (both through consumption and inclusion into the army) and thereby into life – and others that are not, and thus associated with and targeted for death. Finally a perspective beyond a limited scope of intersectionality and the marking of identity categories will point us to other queer political categories, especially the notion of *queer temporality* and a philosophical reflection on how the view to the *queer future* opens up

*

to the political potential of rejecting the here and now as the radical alternative to Fanon's trauma of the endless repetition of *colonial time*.

Chapter 5 introduces the work of Sun Ra, a major quAre artist as I will argue, whose domain is precisely the future and who provides a perspective that goes beyond the status of the victim and slave, establishing a quAre image of the black inventor. A reflection on Sun Ra's non-outed gayness further investigates Ra's quAre identity as well as questions of illness and alien drag. The backdrop for Sun Ra's work is highlighted with a genealogical overview of Afrofuturism. Afrofuturism works through the images of the traumatic past of slavery and turns them around. For a group whose past and present have been radically destroyed, black science fiction opens up a productive ensemble of images and transfigurations. Thus, the slaveship is mirrored through the spaceship and the notion of the non-human, captivated body is reflected through identification with the alien. In a multitude of constellations, the alien gives reference to the kidnapped slaves in the new world but also the inventive creativity of black counter-constructions and fantasies as aliens that are autonomous to the unmarked whiteness of what is considered human. To address the spatial dimension of black science-fiction and visual as well as musical counter-politics, I look at Paul Gilroy's concept of the Black Atlantic, which investigates the traumatic space of the Middle Passage between Africa and the Americas as a hybrid place of resonance, both giving account to past traumas but also to new black sounds and images that neither identify with essentialist understandings of blackness and black nationalism, nor with a rejection of addressing the experience of slavery and exploitation. After all these spatial and temporal backdrops, issues of quAre space and time are further investigated through a close reading of the film *Space Is the Place*, which was produced by director John Coney in collaboration with Sun Ra. *Space Is the Place* also goes beyond the clichés of the black movement-images of Blaxploitation: The film presents a non-linear dimension of time, which I try to highlight through the application of Deleuze's time-image. Furthermore, it also constructs a quAre idea of black emancipation beyond hegemonic forms of black masculinity and authenticity. Concretely, Sun Ra is challenging the idea that the *black macho* could be the right figure of identification for black emancipation. Instead, Sun Ra's questioning of a linear understanding of a black past and black future challenges simplistic claims of inclusion into the notion of the human and the nation. Through the affirmative event of the concert and the performativity of alien drag, Sun Ra poses a radical critique of both humanism and armed struggle. Instead, the concert and its improvized and collective sound politics reach for a place beyond dualisms and simplified identity politics and furthermore are open to include and transform the minds of blacks and whites alike. Chapter 7 further investigates the collective sonic production of the Arkestra through the notion of the assemblage, a connection of practices, instruments, technologies, and bodies that don't place the subject as the only central point of categories and politics. I also look at the collective community of the Arkestra as an alternative to ideas of kinship and the nuclear family and make a case for the inclusion of Sun Ra and other quAre artists into the (mostly unmarked white) canon of the arts and modernity.

*

2.0 Slavery as Epistemological Break in Gender and Queer Studies

*

If we look at gender and queer studies, stemming from the unmarked white feminist and homosexual movements, as a product of the Enlightenment project, it is not a matter of denouncing it (of course not), but it nevertheless has to be confronted with one major contradiction of the Enlightenment project: slavery (and its aftermath). While, as Sabine Broeck points out,[13] gender and queer studies progressively highlight the agency of certain minor subjects (women and queers) into the realm of the human, their unmarked whiteness makes us forget that the whole construction of the European and western subject is still positioned in relation to dehumanized and thereby unmentioned non-western subjects, marked as colored. To paraphrase Broeck, the critical reflection at stake here is to see how the epistemes of the Enlightenment are historically and forcefully bound to the transatlantic, occidental practices of slavery and colonialism. Thereby the relevant intervention is not only to add the category of race as one next to many others (such as gender, sexuality, or class), but to make the history of slavery a primary perspective for an epistemological intervention into the mostly unmarked gender-race relations of the similarly unmarked whiteness of gender and queer studies.[14]

---

[13] Here I'm following some of Susanne Broecks basic arguments in her noteworthy text "Das Subjekt der Aufklärung – Sklaverei – Gender Studies: Zu einer notwendigen Relektüre der Moderne," *Gender Kontrovers – Genealogien und Grenzen einer Kategorie*, ed. Gabriele Dietze and Sabine Hark (Königstein/Taunus: Ulrike Helmer Verlag, 2006)152-180.

[14] Another noteworthy book about the intersections of sexuality, race and colonialism has to be mentioned here. In Ann Laura Stoler's *Race and the Education of Desire*, Foucault's legendary study about sexuality gets confronted with similar complicated power dimensions of "race" that are also at the center of debate here. See Ann Laura Stoler, *Race and the Education of Desire: Foucault's History of Sexuality and the Colonial Order of Things* (Durham: Duke University Press: 1995).

*

The central contradiction of the Enlightenment can be easily described when looking at Hegel's universal ontology, an ontology that even metaphorically included the striking example of the binding relation of master and slave and an idealized way to the universal freedom of the subject, but which didn't include even one sentence about the fundamental power exchange between whites and blacks in the high time of slavery. As Susan Buck-Morss elaborates in her important text *Hegel, Haiti, and Universal History*:

> By the eighteenth century, slavery had become the root metaphor for Western political philosophy, connoting everything that was evil about power relations. Freedom, its conceptual antithesis, was considered by Enlightenment thinkers as the highest and universal value. Yet this political metaphor began to take root at precisely the time that the economic practice of slavery — the systematic, highly sophisticated capitalist enslavement of non-Europeans as a labor force in the colonies — was increasing qualitatively to the point that by the mid-eighteenth century it came to underwrite the entire economic system of the West, paradoxically facilitating the global spread of the very Enlightenment ideals that were in such fundamental contradiction to it.[15]

Buck-Morss underscores that this problematic paradox is not an exception, but also can be found, for example, in Locke, Rousseau, and Diderot. Furthermore she makes us aware that slavery not only happened on the plantations, but has to be understood as a violent,

---

15 Susan Buck-Morss, *Hegel, Haiti, and Universal History* (Pittsburgh: University of Pittsburgh Press, 2009), 21.

*

multi-faceted deployment that includes kidnapping and forced labor, exploitation of bodies and territories, surveillance and scientific experiments, based on the distinction of non-western bodies, marked as colored. As Broeck notes:

> The equation "non-white = slave = dishonorable and alienated from his birthright = socially dead," which does have its impact far beyond actual slavery until today, allowed modernity to carry a fatal degree of human objectivation and abjection with itself.[16]

From this point of view Broeck notes that gender studies are still dealing with some sort of Eurocentric narcissism. While, for instance, the separation of nature and culture, domestic and public labor has been rightly criticized by white feminism, advocating freedom and being paid for work, such as the work that a mother does at home, the transatlantic dimension of modernity involving the dehumanizing abuse, theft, and killing of bodies has largely not been addressed. The private sphere, for example, which has classically been addressed as a *feminized* space of unpaid labor, *is still* a privileged space of white womanhood, as the slaves could not own a private space of reproduction in the same sense at all. In her important text "Mama's Baby, Papa's Maybe," Hortense Spillers makes the distinction between body and flesh; liberated and captivated subject positions, brutal distinctions untold in the self-referential narrative of white gender studies. In a sense, slaves were not part of the symbolic order of gender difference that established itself in the New World. As Spillers elaborates:

> That order, with its human sequence written in blood, represents for its African and indigenous peoples a sense of

---

16 Broeck 157, translated by the author.

*

> actual mutilation, dismemberment, and exile. First of all, their New-World, diasporic plight marked a theft of the body — a willful and violent … severing of the captive body from its motive will, its active desire. Under these conditions, we lose at least gender difference in the outcome, and the female body and the male body become a territory of cultural and political maneuver, not at all gender related, gender specific.[17]

From this perspective, the first category that I will build my arguments on will be race and with it, the constitutive dualism of whiteness and blackness, as a constitutive ground to expand my later arguments in relation to the intersectional categories of gender and sexuality. But first I'll turn my attention to Frantz Fanon, one of the groundbreaking thinkers of postcolonialism and somebody who precisely takes up the constitutive contradiction of Hegel's ontology when he directly addresses the black experience.

---

17 Spillers 67.

2.1 Fanon and the Black Experience

> Oh my body, make me always a man who questions![18]

Frantz Fanon wrote a whole chapter on "The Lived Experience of the Black Man"[19] in his groundbreaking work *Black Skins, White Masks*,[20] which was one of the founding books on blackness and whiteness, colonialism and slavery. Drawing influence from thinkers such as Sartre and Hegel, Fanon didn't overlook the fact that Hegel's ontology had the potential to address universal freedom, while at the same time ignoring the realities of slavery and thereby, the black experience. Therefore, Fanon made this unspoken relationality between white master and black slave the center of his ontology of "the black man": "Ontology does not allow us to understand the being of the black man, since it ignores the lived experience. For not only must the black man be black; he must be black in relation to the white man."[21]

Therefore, for Fanon, there is no natural or pre-given essence and meaning to blackness itself. The black self in the modern world simply doesn't exist beyond the interpellations by the white master, the slave owner, or the colonialist conqueror. Thus, the white gaze and colonial ideology constitute the black subject's being. In a sense,

---

18 Frantz Fanon, *Black Skin, White Masks* (New York: Grove Press, 2008) 206.
19 Fanon, *Black Skin, White Masks* 89.
20 Fanon, *Black Skin, White Masks* 89-120.
21 Fanon, *Black Skin, White Masks* 90. One has to mention though that his ontologic setup is based on masculinity. Also, his further analysis of black and white gender relations, sexuality and desire are problematic. However, when it comes to the analysis of black appearance under the white gaze, I think Fanon's analysis is still very helpful.

the black man is an object of a meaning that is inscribed on his body and projected onto his representation: "I am overdetermined from the outside... I am a slave not to the 'idea' others have of me, but to my appearance."[22]

A classic example in Fanon's writing is the moment when a white child shouts: "Look! A Negro!"[23] Here the experience of the black body itself is already alienated and experienced as a burden. As Judith Butler elaborates, through the interpellative act connecting naming and seeing, "the 'look' is both a pointing and a seeing, a pointing out what there is to see, a pointing which circumscribes a dangerous body, a racist indicative which relays its own danger to the body to which it points."[24] Fanon describes the confrontation with the white gaze through the physical metaphor of an "unusual weight":

> ...then we were given the occasion to confront the white gaze. An unusual weight descended on us. The real world robbed us our share. In the white world, the man of color encounters difficulties in elaborating his body schema. The image of one's body is solely negating. It's an image in the third person. All around the body reigns an atmosphere of certain uncertainty.[25]

The alienation of the black's body that is overwritten by racialized meaning goes so far that the black corporeal experience is even felt

---

[22] Fanon, *Black Skin, White Masks* 95.
[23] Fanon, *Black Skin, White Masks* 90.
[24] Judith Butler, "Endangered Endangering – Schematic Racism and White Paranoia," *The Judith Butler Reader*, ed. Sara Salih with Judith Butler, (Malden/Oxford: Blackwell Publishing, 2004) 204-212, here 207.
[25] Fanon, *Black Skin, White Masks* 90.

*

in the smallest movements: the motoric experience of the body is disowned. Even grabbing a cigarette can result in estrangement and loss of control regarding one's own body-schemata:

> A slow construction of my self as a body in the middle of a spatial and temporal world — which seems to be the schema... Beneath a body schema I had created a historical-racial schema. The data I used were provided not by 'remnants of feelings and notions of the tactile, vestibular, kinesthetic, or visual nature' but by the Other, the white man, who had woven me out of a thousand details, anecdotes, and stories. [26]

These narratives are not only superficial discourses and banal prejudices. On the contrary, these stories continue narrating one of the most traumatic backsides of modernity through racist stereotyping. While the Enlightenment in Europe was being announced, it seemed deeply natural that the same people who announced freedom would colonize the rest of the world and own slaves, not to speak of the exploitation of the colonized land and along with it the products of coffee, tea, or cacao. This was only possible through a radical distinction between the white human and the black animal and is underlined by the endless stories of black minoriority, a narrative that went on for centuries. Fanon comments:

---

26 Fanon, *Black Skin, White Masks* 92.

> I was responsible not only for my body but also for my race and my ancestors. I cast an objective gaze over myself, discovered my blackness, my ethnic features; deafened by cannibalism, backwardness, fetishism, racial stigmas, slave traders...[27]

In a moving description Fanon underlines how discourses not only form exterior exclusion but interior physical distortions as well. The trauma of the endlessly repeating racist narrative forms a vicious circle and makes even the body collapse: "...the body schema, attacked in several places, collapsed."[28] In another example, Fanon is looking for a place in a train. He experiences how the whites leave several rows free between them, and any move towards them provokes further reactions of distanciation: "I approached the other ... and the other, evasive, hostile, but not opaque, vanished. Nausea."[29] Again we can see how racism is experienced directly in a physical realm. It affects the deepest impulses of the body — a dimension of corporeal affectivity that has been mostly ignored when dealing with body politics. Maybe one day an intersection of queer, critical race, and dis/ability studies will be able to grasp these affects in the political complexity that is shown here by Fanon, who himself worked as a psychiatrist in France and Algeria and was one of the first theorists to analyze the interface of the effects of racism and psychological suffering, a suffering that seemed to have no end and represents a vicious circle:

---

27 Fanon, *Black Skin, White Masks* 92.
28 Ibid.
29 Ibid.

*

> The circuit thereby created seems to be closed — there is no possibility of a conception of a future that could be different from the colonial past.... For the living being who is recognized a priori as black according to a collective conception of blackness, the present is simply affect, a sensory perception that is the arrested action of the past on the present.[30]

When slavery was abolished in the US, which started at the beginning of the nineteenth century, obviously racism didn't end. A lot of racial discrimination not only survived in the material class positions of black labor, but was also redistributed through culture. Freak-shows and circuses, postcards and paintings, games and consumer products made the old traumatic images of the savage, the monster and the obedient but happy servant continue to live on. From a temporal perspective, there was still no way to a thinkable future of blackness. As Kara Keeling notes, "the past traumas of colonization and slavery continue to affect and shape the present at the expense of the black's future liberation."[31]

Picture of Frantz Fanon (1925-1961)

---

30 Keeling 33.
31 Ibid.

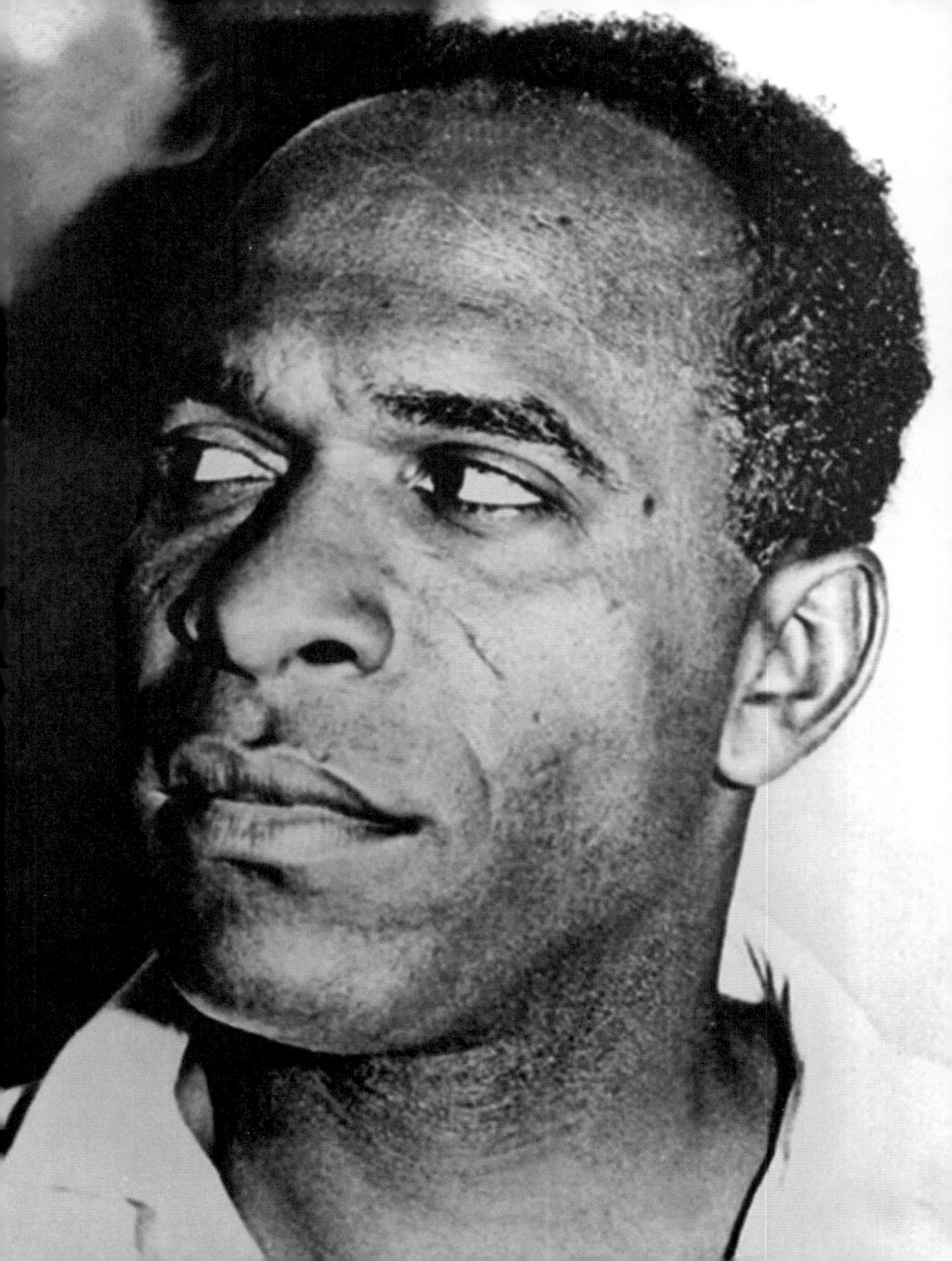

2.2 Fanon in the Cinema, Waiting

> The black man is a toy in the hands of the white man. So in order to break the vicious circle, he explodes. I can't go to the movies without encountering myself. I wait for myself. Just before the film starts, I wait for myself.... My aching heart makes my head spin.[32]

In this quote Fanon powerfully relates the racism of representation in post-slavery times to the cinema and the passivity of the viewer who is exposed to the discourse of the whites. During the interval, after the commercials and before the main feature, Fanon's heart already makes his head spin in anticipation that the always same images of "the negro" might appear. The trauma of colonialism plays out in the fear and experience of endless repetition.

But let's keep in mind that the moment of waiting in the interval also includes a moment of in-betweenness, an ambivalence of uncertainty about what will happen, a minor potentiality that another image, another time might appear: "Perhaps a whole other reality — one that we do not yet have a memory of as such — opens up."[33]

At the beginning of the quote though, Fanon also mentions the potential of a violent, yet revolutionary force that could make the black break free from the vicious circle of colonial time: "... in order to break the vicious circle, he explodes." While white racist discourses always tried to represent the black as a *public danger* and therefore

---

32 Fanon, *Black Skin, White Masks* 119.
33 Keeling 40.

provide reasons to put him behind bars, here, the black himself also might become a danger for the white men's sovereignity.[34]

2.3 The Black Danger and the White Nation

Before we look at the subversive potential of the *black danger* or the *explosive black*, however, we will look into a primary example of racist, yet canonical cinema from film history, to analyze the trauma of visuality that Fanon described. A black man running through the streets – this moment of free movement and agency after the abolition of slavery, has never stopped troubling the white man. To see the intensity of this paradigmatic "white paranoia," we can look to D.W. Griffith's classic work *Birth of a Nation* (1915), which provides examples that are as striking as they are humiliating. It is worth noting that *Birth of a Nation* was the most successful film of the silent era, admired for its dynamics and stylistic originality, even though its content was obviously far from being modern[35] and was full of racist revisionism[36].

---

34 Even if I base my analysis on the explosive black and the dualism of black and white, it is worth noting that Homi Bhabha's reading of Fanon tries to undo the dualism of black and white as pure radical opposites – instead, Bhabha proposes the notion of ambivalence that doesn't have to be confined to the negativity of the explosion. See Homi Bhabha, "What does the Black Man Want?" *New Formations, Remembering Fanon*, London: No. 1, Spring 1987.
35 http://en.wikipedia.org/wiki/The_Birth_of_a_Nation
36 Obviously *Birth of a Nation* is only one of the most extreme examples. Racist revisionism has many ways. Another example that should at least be mentioned is *Gone with the Wind* by Victor Fleming (1939), which could be seen as a softcore version of the same problematic discourses. It would take until the seventies (of course there are exceptions) before slavery was represented in all its problematics. Television was an especially successful format for doing this, perhaps because there is another temporal dimension of storytelling at work which is not restricted, quantitatively nor qualitatively, by the limits of the feature film. See, for instance, *Roots* (various directors, 1979) and *Queen* (John Erman, 1993), both based on novels by Afro-American writer Alex Haley.

Theatrical poster for *Birth of a Nation* (1915)

*

In the narrative, the notorious Ku Klux Klan becomes an American rescue army against the "backward blacks" who seem to threaten the communal foundation of the United States. Thus, the film is one of the major revisionist works that provides reasons that the US needs a white army to put the *black danger* back in its place. "No single film in the silent era is more important to the critical history of stereotype than is D.W. Griffith's *Birth of a Nation*," writes film theorist Robyn Wiegman.[37] One scene specifically relates the black man moving through open space with the notion of a *black danger* and the stigma of the monster. The soldier and "freedman" Gus (Walter Long) is represented as a suspicious stranger hanging around in front of a white family's house. Happy that he became a captain in the American army, he seems to feel somewhat included in the national community and even tries to flirt with a white woman. He meets the white female character Flora Cameron (Mae Marsh) in the woods, where she is following the movements of a squirrel. She is fascinated by the animal, depicting her as both innocent and close to nature.[38] Gus moves towards her and excitedly announces: "You see, I'm a captain now – and I want to marry." Then he tries to touch Flora's hand. Flora immediately feels harassed and gives him a slap in the face. Then she runs away. After announcing his peaceful ambitions – "Wait missie, I won't hurt yeh." – Gus runs after her and is directly put into a classic scene of white paranoia, where the black, again, only functions as a danger to the white and in this case, to feminine nature-like innocence. Back in the scene, Gus further follows her through the

---

[37] See Robyn Wiegman, "Race, Ethnicity and Film," *The Oxford Guide to Film Studies*, ed. John Hill and Pamela Church Gibson (Oxford: Oxford University Press, 1998) 158-168.

[38] Obviously, but worth noting – a classic sexist stereotype that divides *women* and *men* like nature and culture.

*

woods, already symbolizing the monster or even the potential rapist that is following his victim. Their "hunt" ends in front of a cliff. Finally, Flora jumps (or falls) down the cliff and dies. The following intertitle comments: "For her who had learned the stern lesson of honor, we should not grieve that she found the sweeter opal gates of death." Even without the notion of any violent action, Gus seems to be made responsible for her dying, while the intertitle even supports her possible jump from the cliff, since not having sexual contact with a black man would have saved her pride. Her brother finds her and wipes her bloody brow with the Confederate flag. Just a few scenes later, Gus is caught, tried, and finally killed by the KKK.

In this framework, the black and white aesthetics of silent cinema strengthen the contrast of visual meanings that are already placed on the black and white characters. Afro-British theorist Kobena Mercer underlines the intensification of the significance of black skin, which can be loaded with both negrophobic or negrophiliac meanings: "Harsh contrasts of shadow and light draw the eye to focus and fix attention on the texture of the black man's skin. According to Bhabha ... skin color functions as '*the most visible of fetishes.*'"[39] While Gus is depicted as a monster who cannot control his desire and who threatens the innocent balance of nature represented through the white woman, the killing of Gus by the Ku Klux Klan symbolizes a righteous intervention to reinstall law and order. Robyn Wiegman elaborates: "Here, the late nineteenth-century image of the African American male as rapist turns to pure spectacle in the ideologically

---

39 Kobena Mercer, *Welcome to the Jungle: New Positions in Black Cultural Studies* (New York: Routledge, 1994) 183.

*

weighted aesthetics of black-and-white film."[40] As Judith Butler made clear in her text "Endangered Endangering – Schematic Racism and White Paranoia," the ideology of the *black danger* has stayed with us to this day. She underscores that the very act of looking itself is never innocent and that it is always already racialized – the white gaze and its projections on blackness already establish what can be seen, and meaning is applied to the imagery: "The visual field is not neutral to the question of race; it is itself a racial formation, an episteme, hegemonic and forceful." Looking therefore becomes "the racial production of the visible, the workings of racial constraints of what it means to see."[41] Her example is the infamous Rodney King case. In 1991, the drunk driver Rodney King was trying to flee from the police and was so brutally attacked that it caused a public uproar. The video of the attack was used in the court case as paradoxical proof that King was a *danger* to the public, even though there was no aggressive act that he ever committed and no weapon in his hand that would support the claim. As if the blackness in the black and white surveillance-video would have proven anything by itself, King was indirectly blamed for being a *monster* and a *danger* to public space.

40 Wiegman 162.
41 Butler 206.

*

As Butler, who also referenced Fanon in her analysis, underscores, a vicious circle is in motion in the case of Rodney King. She takes up Fanon's notion of the *historico-racial schema*, in her words a *racist episteme*:

> The video was used as "evidence" to support the claim that the frozen black male body on the ground receiving blows was himself producing those blows, about to produce them, was himself the imminent threat of a blow and, therefore, was himself responsible for the blows he received. That body thus received those blows in return for the ones it was about to deliver, the blows which were that body in its essential gestures, even as the one gesture that body can be seen to make is to raise its palm outward to stave off the blows against it. According to this racist episteme, he is hit in exchange for the blows he never delivered, but which he is, by virtue of his blackness, always about to deliver.... This is an action that the black male body is always already performing within that white racist imaginary, has always already performed prior to the emergence of any video.[42]

---

42 Butler 207-208.

Gus being caught by the KKK. Film still from *Birth of a Nation*

*

2.4 The Sexualization of Racism

Kobena Mercer analyzes this sexualized economy of the visual and the fixation of the black, who is supposed to be a danger, rapist or monster as a form of white fetishism, which marks the black, supposed to be in possession of a too big penis, as a bad object. He also emphasizes that white paranoia about the black male was already addressed in Fanon's writings:

> As a phobic object, the big black prick is a "bad object", a fixed point in the paranoid fantasies of the negrophobe which Fanon found in the pathologies of his white psychiatric patients as much as in the normalized cultural artifacts of this time. Then, as now…one is no longer aware of the Negro, but only of a penis; the Negro is eclipsed. He is turned into a penis. He is a penis.[43]

In this sense the black phallus marks a powerful racist stereotype in white people's fantasies. But it is not only white paranoid projection on black *masculinity* that has been sexualized. Similarly, black *femininity* has been racified and sexualized by the white gaze. A classic example is the story of the "Hottentot Venus" Saartje Baartman, also known as Sarah Bartmann. The Khoisan woman was born in Kaffraria, an Eastern Cape Colony of South Africa in the 1780s. When her homeland came under Dutch colonial rule, she worked as a slave at the Cape of Good Hope. After some time, she entered into an agreement with the colonialists Peter Cezar and Alexander Dunlop to travel with them to Britain. There she worked not only as a domestic helper but also would be exhibited in England and Ireland because of her supposedly "larger than 'normal'"

---

[43] Mercer 185.

*

buttocks.[44] So here we go again: While the myth of the big genitals of *black men* still circulates in, for instance, contemporary pornography, as titles such as *Blackzilla*[45] obviously suggest, the freak show would also produce its own racial pornography back in the day. Again, as in Baartman's case, the size of her genitals and buttocks would be the reason to *exhibit* her, and like in the male's case, this would also produce assumptions about her *animal-like* sexuality. In colonial ideology, her exposedness and nudity were linked with the projection of gaining knowledge about her. An example worth mentioning is the case of the French naturalist and anatomist Georges Cuvier, whose "examination" of Baartman brought him to the "great discovery" of the "Hottentot Apron" (the hypertrophy of the labia minora) and the "abnormality" of Baartman's "smaller pelvis." As Obioma Nnaemeka underlines:

> Cuvier saw this abnormality as another sign of the Black Woman's primitivism. He also found Baartman's pelvis to be smaller and less flared than the white woman's and resembles more the pelvis of a female monkey. Bartman's racial difference denoted her below human level and linked her to other social outcasts such as lesbians and prostitutes.[46]

---

44 Obioma Nnaemeka (2005), "Bodies That Don't Matter: Black Bodies and the European Gaze," *Mythen, Masken und Subjekte. Kritische Weißseinsforschung in Deutschland*, ed. Eggers et al. (Münster: Unrast Verlag, 2005) 98-99.

45 See, for instance, *My Mom is Fucking Blackzilla*: http://tour.mymomsfuckingblackzilla.com/ As "Blackzilla" and other *ethnic* porn lines remind us, in a time of queer pornography and a fair amount of feminist representations in the genre, the matter of race is less often touched and addressed to be criticized and deconstructed. To follow Maxime Cervulle, a post-exotic pornography is still a marginal concept that queer and anti-racist porn-producers and activists have to find better strategies for. See Maxime Cervulle, "Erotic / Exotic. Race and Class in French Gay 'Ethnic' Pornography," *Post/Porn/Politics*, 180-189.

46 Nnaemeka 99.

*

As Roderick Ferguson points out, in post-slavery times, the ideology surrounding racist projections on black women's sexuality would continue to culminate in the image of the black prostitute:

> In fact, nineteenth-century iconography used the image of ... Bartmann ... to link the figure of the prostitute to the alleged sexual savagery of black women to install non-white sexuality as the axis upon which various notions of womanhood turned. As industrial capital developed and provided working-class white women with limited income and mobility, the prostitute became the racialized figure that could enunciate anxieties about such changes.[47]

In her noteworthy study, Siobhan B. Somerville has argued that race and sexuality have long been intrinsically linked in white racist discourses. It is therefore not possible to understand the intersectional power mechanisms coming into play here by "just" looking at one category of power. In her book *Queering the Color Line: Race and the Invention of Homosexuality in American Culture*[48] she makes clear that the legal categories of race and sexuality in the United States were basically established at the same time — at the end of the nineteenth century[49]:

---

47 Roderick A. Ferguson, *Aberrations in Black: Towards a Queer of Color Critique* (Minneapolis: University of Minnesota Press, 2004) 9.
48 Siobhan B. Somerville, *Queering the Color Line: Race and the Invention of Homosexuality in American Culture* (Durham: Duke University Press, 2000).
49 To add another historical intersection, this was also the time when the photographic apparatus was invented and cinema became established as a form of mass entertainment.

*

> ...although some scholarship has drawn parallels between discourses of racial difference and sexuality, their particular relationship and potentially mutual effects remain largely unexplored.... I show that it was not merely a historical incidence that the classification of bodies as either "homosexual" or "heterosexual" emerged at the same time that the United States was aggressively constructing and policing the boundary between "black" and "white" bodies.... I argue ... that the simultaneous efforts to shore up and bifurcate categories of race and sexuality in the late nineteenth and early twentieth centuries were deeply intertwined.[50]

Literature by medical, physical, psychological, and academic "experts" would serve as leading guidelines for American citizens. Books like Havelock Ellis's *Studies in Psychology of Sex* were supposed to help and lead the white middle-class citizen into a "non-pathological" everyday life. As Ellis wrote: "I regard sex as the central problem of life.... the question of sex — with the racial questions that rest on it — stands before the coming generations as the chief problem for solution."[51]

---

50 Somerville 3-4.
51 Quoted in Somerville 5.

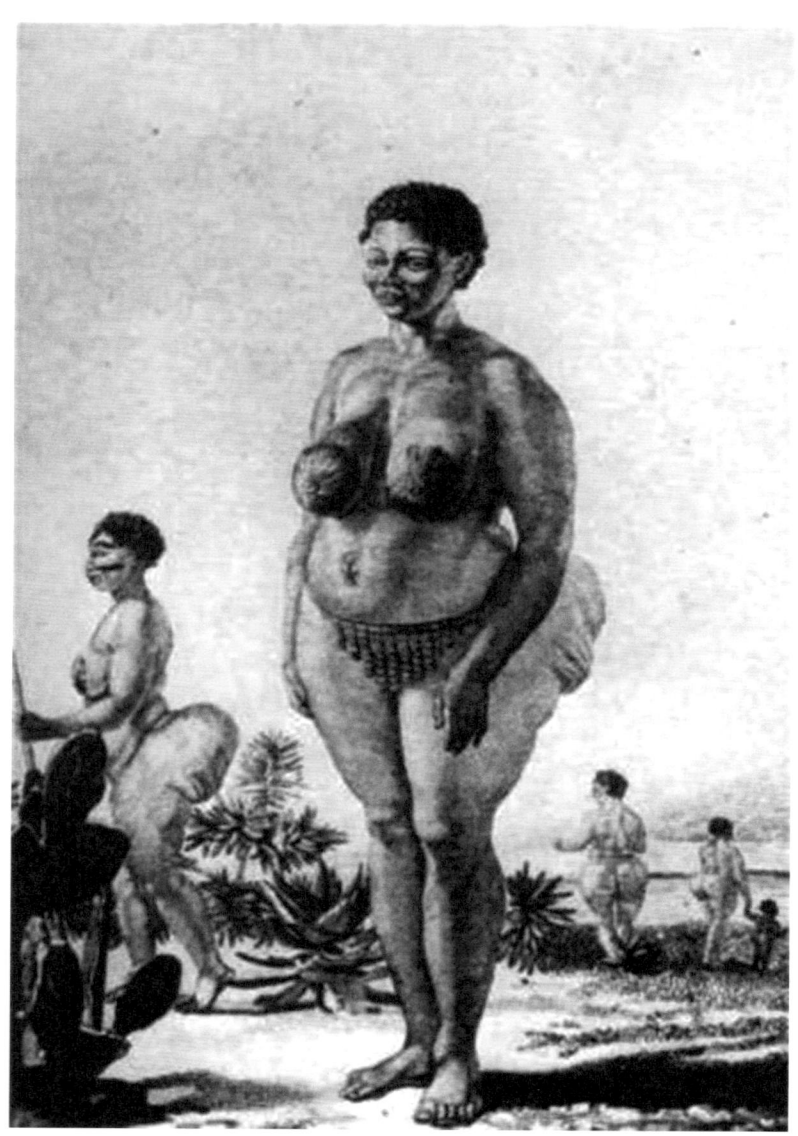

Saartje Baartman, the "Hottentot Venus"

So while blackness was pathologized in relation to white normativity, homosexuality was pathologized in relation to heterosexual normativity. Therefore, if heterosexual or homosexual, one might think about the possibility that black sexuality has already been labeled somewhat queer and was considered dangerous and destabilizing to normative white sexualities.

Furthermore, both gender and race discourses would culminate in interlocked definitions of queer bodies. While, for instance, Saartje Baartman would shock because of the size of her genitals, even many years later white parents would argue for a color separation in school because they were scared of the too masculine, supposedly lesbian black girls that would homosexualize their children.[52] In this sense there are multiple intersections and interfaces between scientific racism and homophobia. It would take until the sixties for the black *danger*, in Fanon's sense, to become *explosive*, and, in Somerville's sense, sexual – and to become appropriated by people of color themselves for the first steps of agency.

*

---

52 Somerville 34.

3.0 Black Films with Blacks with Guns

*

Page 49, *Cock and Gun* (1982).
Photo by the white, gay artist Robert Mapplethorpe

With the beginning of the Black Power Movement, a new image of blackness would finally appear and intervene into the American public realm. In a way, the helpless passivity of the black which Fanon described as he was waiting in the cinema was broken by the circulation of the media representations of activist groups like the Black Panther Party, which intervened in the visual public sphere with a strong performativity. If we follow the image of the armed, *dangerous*, and thereby *explosive* African American, we can see how its main characteristics were taken up and would circulate in newspapers and in radio and television news. These images, as I will argue inspired by the work of black queer theorist Kara Keeling, were the basis of a visual politics that transformed into the first black American cinema: Blaxploitation. This cinema would intervene into the power apparatus of white cinema and change the sense of black self-representation into a more empowered, affirmative event. This event of emancipated blackness would then also produce a black audience that would feel empowered and therefore be able to perform an autonomous black movement and therefore, another black future.

The Blaxploitation genre would feature black main characters that not only survive the narrative of the film, but also pose an alternative to the hegemonic outcome of being lynched. Furthermore it would help to construct counter-images to white common sense, as the (anti-) heroes of Blaxploitation would represent deviant forms of life and would question the rule of the white police representing the nation state. In this sense, the images of the Black Panthers and other black

*

emancipatory organizations, which represented the ongoing Black Liberation struggle of the late sixties and early seventies, marked an epistemological break with the hegemonic and racist representation of blackness.

For Kara Keeling, the appropriation of the stereotypes of the *dangerous black with a gun* constituted the Blaxploitation genre and later was updated in the ghetto-centric cinema.[53] In Blaxploitation the *dangerous* black would pose resistance to racist stereotypes and actions and fight for his right to move freely through public space. Therefore, in these films the black movement really became a struggle for black movement. Daniel Kreiss describes the symbolic power of the weapon not being owned by white cops alone any more, but by the Black Panthers themselves. In this context it is worth noting that Black Panther leaders such as Huey P. Newton were very aware of the performative power of the gun.[54] While the Panthers obviously would have lost a real civil war with the American army, Newton's hope was that the performative dimension of the armed Panthers would still construct a symbolic counterpower to hegemony. In this sense a *real* armed struggle was secondary for Black Liberation, while militant performative aesthetics became one key for it.[55] As Kreiss notes:

---

53 See Keeling 95-137.
54 In his striking essay Kreiss not only demonstrates analogies and differences between the *Panthers* and Sun Ra, but also underlines the performative power of the weapon. See Daniel Kreiss "Appropriating the Master's Tools: Sun Ra, the Black Panthers, and Black Consciousness, 1952-1973," *Black Music Research Journal*, Vol. 28, No.1, Spring (2008): 70.
55 For a wider analysis of black style politics from 1943 to 1975 see Philipp Dorestal, *Style Politics: Mode, Geschlecht und Schwarzsein in den USA, 1943-1975* (Bielefeld: Transcript Verlag, 2012).

*

> It was through these performances that the gun became a tool for the creation of revolutionary consciousness in the minds of the black masses. The gun was viewed as a prosthesis of the human body... that was only imbued with meaning through its reconception in a performative context.[56]

Thus, the distribution of the *performance of the gun* in visual media by the Black Panthers produced Blaxploitation and along with it the black movement-image.

---

56 Kreiss 70.

Blacks with Guns: Black Panther leaders Eldrige Cleaver and Huey P. Newton (with a gun in his hand)

3.1 A Minoritarian Cinema: The Black Movement-Image

Blaxploitation films were b-movies, a kind of working class Hollywood, which consisted of small budget productions that were screened in minor cinemas on the outskirts of the cities. A poor, and here most notably black audience would visit the cinemas after working hours to find some distraction from everyday life. From the perspective of Deleuze, a minoritarian cinema is precisely a subversive cinema, as it challenges hegemony without taking the place of a dominant, leading force like the leading sergeant would take in the army. Deleuze liked cinema and produced a philosophy proper to it. For him, the hierarchy between high art and low trash had to be challenged, and cinema was one of its most successful forms. He therefore makes no qualitative difference between physics and philosophy, painting, music, or film – for him all of these contexts are similarly able to invent ideas and produce concepts. As Keeling notes: "For Deleuze, cinema is a mode of thinking, that is, of creating concepts. Excavating and encouraging alternative ways of knowing and thinking requires the creation and adoption of new concepts and paradigms."[57]

However, very different from the way his philosophical ethics of multiplicity usually works, Deleuze's film history, which is elaborated through the books *Cinema I: The Movement-Image* and *Cinema II: The Time-Image*, convey a very linear narrative of historical progression. The first book starts at the historical beginning of cinema and the second stops in the middle of the eighties, which makes it seem as if there were a natural progression of the medium, unchallenged by more multidimensional ruptures and perspectives. Also, Deleuze's

---

57 Keeling 5.

*

cinema books, as well as his whole philosophy, sometimes mention perspectives of color but rarely give them their own political space. One example among many is that Deleuze fails to contextualize and give account to the political relevance of the positions of people of color. Keeling formulates this critique very directly when discussing Deleuze's whole body of work: "Deleuze himself is notorious for having little or nothing to say about race."[58]

Still, his concept of minoritarian politics is perfectly suitable to describe the politically subversive position and practice that Blaxploitation cinema embodies. Deleuze constructed the notion of the minor in relation to writers like Kafka, who wrote in a major language (German) that wasn't his own (he was Czech) and who used it for a writing that both undermined the official form of its usage and produced concepts that challenged, in Kafka's case, both the German language as well as the way to write stories, not to mention his singular characters that challenge the dualism of the human and the animal.

Deleuze was also influenced by the different minoritarian struggles of 1968, be it by students and workers, or feminists, homosexuals, or persons of color. The minoritarian doesn't work in antagonism to the majoritarian (as a political party would), but it undermines hegemonic centers and produces new molecular connections between thought, experience, and practice. It also challenges classic dialectical critiques of the negative and engages in more inventive acts than

---

[58] Keeling 5. However, there are contemporary examples that show Deleuze's thought can be applied to questions of postcolonialism or non-western "world" cinema: See: David Martin-Jones, ed., *Deleuze and World Cinemas* (London: Continuum, 2010) and Simone Bignall and Paul Patton, eds., *Deleuze and the Postcolonial* (Edinburgh: Edinburgh University Press, 2010).

*

cultural pessimism or war. For Deleuze, the minor is also driven by desire and affirmation. In this sense, "Black is Beautiful" is a minor positive statement that affirms difference from a minor point of view, which also engages with the white hegemonic language of the post-slavery states of America to create new connections with the oppressed, posing an alternative, for example, to "Look! A Negro!" — the traumatic interpellation that Frantz Fanon described. Constantine Verevis notes that a minor cinema goes beyond representing oppression and invents another future for the subjects in question. He cites three points that make the notion of a minor cinema concrete:

> First, a minor cinema does not represent (or address) an oppressed and subjected people, but rather anticipates a people yet to be created, a consciousness to be brought into existence. Second, a minor cinema does not maintain a boundary between the private and the public, but rather crosses borders, merging the personal with the social to make it immediately political. And third, recognizing that the people exist only in the condition of a minority, political cinema does not identify a new union (a singularity) but rather creates (and recreates) a multiplicity of condition.[59]

All three of these points were present in Blaxploitation film when it came to life in the early seventies. Instead of making the black experience only one of the victims, it represented black main characters that would be successful in fighting for a new agency. The black passivity of slavery was broken and the vision of Blaxploitation

---

[59] Constantine Verevis, "Minoritarian & Cinema," *The Deleuze Dictionary*, ed. Adrian Parr (Edinburgh: Edinburgh University Press, 2010) 165-167.

included new fashions and haircuts, jokes and statements, styles and performances. In the logics of "Black Is Beautiful!" it did its part to free black subjects from their racialized stigmas. Furthermore it connected supposedly private issues to the political. An Afro haircut would be the sign for black liberation as would be the pop music soundtracks of Curtis Mayfield and Isaac Hayes, which provided further sociopolitical commentary about the emotional landscapes of the black heroes and heroines depicted in the first Afro-American film genre. In a concrete sense, the minoritarian cinema of Blaxploitation also creates, for the first time in a continuous fashion, a black movement-image. Let's recall Fanon and his experience of blackness. The body of the black is not connected to its own movements any more, behind his body schema Fanon encounters a historical-racial schema made up of the fantasies of whites. In this experience, being one with your black body seems impossible, even smoking a cigarette becomes an alienated performance. There seems to be no way that a closed world, in which the black physically functions in sync with his body, can be constructed. It is this disposition that makes Fanon sit passively in the cinema, already worried that the same racist images will appear again. But how would he have reacted if a Blaxploitation film had appeared on the screen? In Blaxploitation, the classic notions of Deleuze's movement-image, movement and editing, character and narration, create a closed and functional world that becomes finally intact precisely *through movement*. Deleuze's concept of the movement-image is based on the philosophy of Henri Bergson. For Bergson, body and brain permanently perceive affects in forms of sensations. Visual affects and sensations are material for Bergson as they reach body and brain through the light that reaches the eye. However, for the body to find a structure for movement, it has to filter out motoric

※

structures from pure sensations. The body is thus able to store images from the past to remember structures of movement in the form of motor mechanisms. When one crosses the street, even if it is a street one has not crossed before, the linear movement is remembered by the body and thus makes one stop at a crossing, look for cars, and follow the proper way. These structural elements that are saved from past experiences, Bergson calls clichés. As Kara Keeling elaborates:

> Clichés provide a way of continuing movement because, in the face of a present perception that affects the sensory elements, they reestablish a relation between the sensory and the motor elements of the sensory-motor schema, allowing for recognition to occur and present movements to continue.[60]

For Deleuze, this process is repeated in the cinema. The light of the projection hits the eye and through the identification with the main character and the functional movements of the narrative in the film space, visual structural clichés are remembered and make the viewer follow the story instead of getting lost in pure visual sensations. So through similarity, the structures already known and saved by the interface of brain and motoric apparatus, narrative continuity, montage and character identification interacting with stored motor memories, the film experience of the movement-image is constituted. For Deleuze, especially in classical Hollywood narrative cinema, the first sixty years of cinema's existence, this is the basic element of cinema.[61] This constitutive structure is precisely the one that

---

60 Keeling 14.
61 In this context it obviously seems more than problematic that the first filmmaker in Deleuze's film books to be mentioned by name is D.W. Griffith. See Gilles Deleuze, *Cinema 1: The Movement-Image* (London: Athlone Press, 1986) 29-32.

*

Fanon describes as being disowned by the black. In this sense, the movement-image gets a new political nuance, unimagined by Deleuze, when Blaxploitation gives rise to the black movement-image, as it is precisely the movements that structure the narrative of the film, and with it, furthermore, a black audience.

Furthermore, the sexualized racism that is projected onto blackness is reversed. What was pathologized and sexualized should become an affirmative tool, not only to criticize police violence, classism, and exclusion, but also to celebrate black vernacular cultures, black sexuality and the struggle for survival of Afro-American identity itself. Also commercially, at least for a few years, Blaxploitation was a success and found its audience. Over 100 films were produced and would influence popular culture as well as real-life struggles.

As we will see, Blaxploitation would start to use the black heterosexual male as a counter-identification but would later also include strong women and queer subtexts. These characters were not innocent heroes, but were shaped by post-slavery history and their class positions. In a country where it was usually only white characters who were the heroes, the Blaxploitation hero obviously represented the ambivalence between hero and anti-hero, between underdog and winner. As Bene Sarraiter puts it, "they are like superheroes, but at the same time they are also antiheroes. A clear border between the hero and the antihero doesn't exist."[62]

---

[62] *Black Dynamite*, dir. Bene Sarreiter, 2011.
See http://www.arte.tv/de/2860746,CmC=2861278.html

*

In its variety, Blaxploitation would provide a necessary black common sense — a cinema that the community identified with and could happily celebrate. In this sense Blaxploitation changed the rules of American cinema. As Keeling notes: "Framed in this way, blaxploitation can be understood as a generic reformation of common-sense black nationalism, that seeks to cut, select, and circulate images of value-in-process capable of a broad circulation."[63]

Already the first Blaxploitation film provides a perfect example for the becoming of the black movement-image. *Sweet Sweetback's Bad Badass Song* was produced in 1970 and written and directed by the black filmmaker Melvin van Peebles. The film became a surprisingly big commercial success[64] and would provide a strong foundation for black common sense, a common sense that would also be deconstructed and challenged with more complex subject constellations in the genre's future. An intersectional analysis of the genre's diversification will provide a genealogical overview of the genre's politics in terms of race, gender, and sexuality.

---

63 Keeling 101.
64 The story of the making and success of *Sweetback* was told in an entertaining manner by Melvin van Peebles's son, Mario von Peebles, in *Badassss*, 2003.

*

3.2 Reading Blaxploitation, Intersectionally

The theory of intersectionality was developed in 1989 by Afro-American feminist and law theorist Kimberlé Williams Crenshaw[65] and has become a major paradigm in feminist, gender, and queer studies. Especially interventions by black feminists have reminded hegemonic feminisms not only that the supposedly universal feminist subject very often stays in the unmarked and unreflected domain of white privileges, but that furthermore, there is not only one subject of womanhood from which a universalist politics can be constructed. Thus, intersectionality poses an alternative to theories and academic disciplines that only concentrate on one identity category to describe exclusion and oppression. Imagine a company where black *men* and white *women* are employed. On the surface this company could promote itself as progressive in the sense of supporting diversity and gender inclusion. Black women, however, are not included in this framework and remain silenced. Kimberle W. Crenshaw used the image of the intersection — a crossing of two streets — to think about, for instance, how gender and race might be intertwined from the perspective of a woman of color, whose positionality in this model is precisely articulated at the point of the crossing itself. As Leslie McCall elaborates:

---

[65] Kimberle Crenshaw, "Demarginalizing the Intersection of Politics and Sex: A Black Feminist Critique of Antidiscrimination Doctrine, Feminist Theory and Antiracist Politics," *The University of Chicago Legal Forum Volume: Theory, Practice and Criticism* (Chicago: University of Chicago Press, 1991) 139-167. However, earlier works, especially of black feminism, had already addressed multiple categories. See, for instance, as already addressed in the title: *Women, Race & Class*, by Angela Davis (London: The Women's Press, 1983).

Interest in intersectionality arose out of a critique of gender-based and race-based research for failing to account for lived experience at neglected points of intersection — ones that tended to reflect multiple subordinate locations as opposed to dominant or mixed locations. It was not possible, for example, to understand a black woman's experience from previous studies of gender combined with previous studies on race because of the distinct and frequently conflicting dynamics that shaped the lived experience of subjects in these social locations.[66]

Furthermore the discussions around intersectionality also opened up a more complex debate about several relevant categories of power and the complexities of producing methodological tools to address double and multiple forms of discrimination between, for instance, categories such as race and ethnicity, gender and sexuality, but also dis/ability and class which are understood to be intrinsically linked and cannot be separated from each other.

As the word intersectionality already makes clear, different axes of power intersect.[67] This chapter will provide a closer look at the intersectional politics of Blaxploitation. While the category race is set as the most important one in the shadow of post-slavery, the categories of gender and sexuality will help us to see how the genre diversified and multiplied its politics of representation.

---

[66] Leslie McCall, "The Complexity of Intersectionality," *Signs: Journal of Women in Culture and Society*, Vol, 30, No. 3. (2005): 1781.
[67] How this important but complex theoretical paradigm can be applied and theorized is still an ongoing discussion. See, for instance, Leslie McCall discussing three different intersectional approaches in "The Complexity of Intersectionality."

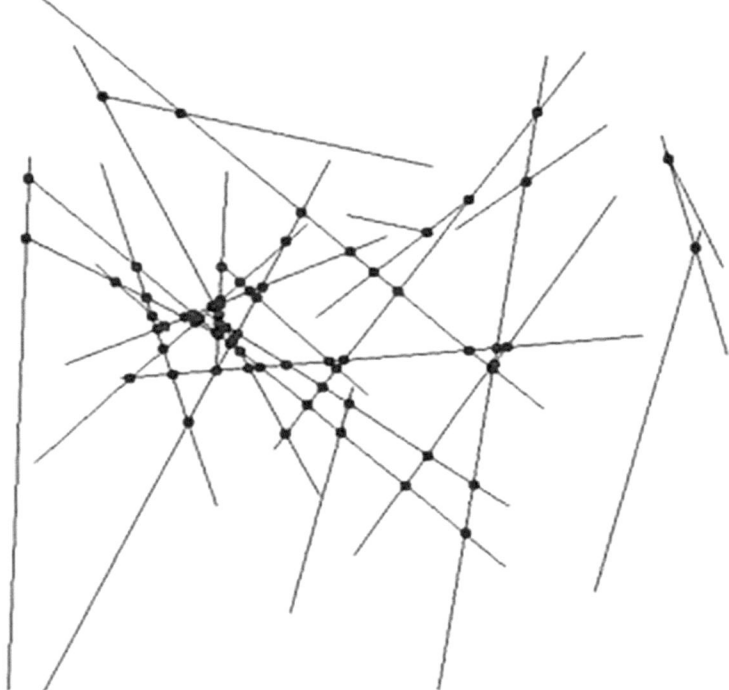

Often the metaphor of the street intersection is used to describe intersectional relations. This is a more complex visualization.

*

As already noted, *Sweet Sweetback's Bad Badass Song* (1970) is the film that started it all. The main character's name Sweetback already highlights that his black bottom is seen in a sweet, thus positive light. He represents the ambivalence of the phallic black: heterosexual, potent, and brought up in a black community of sexworkers. The intersection of race and sexuality already provides a backdrop for his identity within the first early minutes of the narrative. The negative stereotype of the black rapist gets turned into a positive one and his sexual power will produce orgasms for black and white women alike throughout the narrative. Raised in a black sexworker community and also depicted as a drag-performing sexworker himself, Sweetback's character is already established outside the heteronormative patterns of recognizable kinship and reproduction. Also later, when Sweetback gets surrounded and threatened by a white motorcycle gang, he saves his life by having sex with the female leader and making her come. In this sense, the film has deconstructed the foundations of the sexualization of racism by appropriating the figure of the *phallic black*. For this, however, the *black macho* was born as the archetypical Blaxploitation hero. As racism was defeated, a certain form of black phallocracy would become one of the main driving forces of the genre.

As one phallic signifier is the black's penis, the other one is the black's gun. The birth of Blaxploitation would be a little more innocent than the cliché of the black with the weapon. Deviant crime would not be the reason why Sweetback is haunted by the police throughout the narrative, which would construct the main motif of the black man moving through public space like an escape route from slavery. The only crime, as it were, that he is guilty of, is attacking two white policemen as they were trying to beat up a black liberation activist.

*

Therefore his motivation is saving an ally and not harming another person or law without reason. Black liberation, however, is not represented as limited to armed struggle but works through solidarity and the black movement towards freedom. As director Melvin van Peebles notes, the Black Panthers loved the film and made it part of their educational member program.[68]

But Sweetback would not only set standards in terms of paradigmatic themes and motifs of the genre. It also introduced an impressive soundtrack that would form a dialogue with the images and make the viewing experience a deeper one. Much like an ancient Greek chorus, the soundtrack, performed by the popular black funk band "Earth Wind and Fire" (and again, partly composed by the omnipresent Melvin van Peebles) would provide a further commentary on the narrative. For instance, as much as Sweetback is moving through the space performing a literal line of flight from imprisonment, a voice would repeatedly appear, commenting: "Come on feet, move for me!" And finally, as Sweetback crosses the Mexican border and successfully overcomes the danger posed by the white American police, a gospel choir makes us remember that before Sweetback's story there have been many black people that were not as lucky as he is: "They bled your mother! They bled your father! They bled your sister!" – to which Sweetback answers: "But they won't bleed me!"

68 See the interview with Melvin van Peebles in *Baadasssss Cinema* by Isaac Julien, 2002.

On the run: Melvin van Peebles as *Sweetback*

*

One has to remember that in these years in American cinema, blacks would only appear as threatening monsters or obedient servants. If they refused to follow the direction of white law, they would usually be punished by the narrative and be dead at the end of the movie. It comes as no surprise that Sweetback was written, produced, and directed by a black filmmaker. As Melvin van Peebles recalls in the documentary *Baad Badass Cinema*:

> I go into the theater. And the theater is packed… Toward the end of the movie… I sit down next to an old black lady and she said: Oh lord let him die. Don't let them kill him. Let him die on his own! It was off her chart that a negro, a colored, a black African American, one of us, would make it until the end of the movie. Cause we didn't make it until the end of the movie…[69]

In this sense Blaxploitation not only opens up a positive representation of black mobility. Through the survival of the hero, the film implies that black people also have a future.[70] In the following years Blaxploitation would become part of the program of popular cinema. Sometimes even the titles of the films implied the heroes' ability to move, such as in *Superfly* (1972). The deviant, phallic *black with the gun* also became the archetype of the genre, living a life in the

---

[69] *Baad Badasssss Cinema*, 2002.
[70] Even if *Sweetback* established the black movement-image, there are many moments in the film that already move beyond the framework of movement and montage, creating sense through the main character and narrative. Sometimes looking like an ode to black mobility itself, the film dwells in musical feedbacks and abstract cut-ups of urban movement itself. From a Deleuzian point of view the film also presents pure sensations of cinema, not bound by story or psychology, but opening up to the whole experience of both black mobility and black image production. In this sense, *Sweetback* is a fascinating hybrid between a genre film and an experimental art film resembling the early works of, for instance, Jean-Luc Godard.

*

underground, sometimes fighting for the police, sometimes against it. As in any process of commercialization and the production of a black common sense,[71] the genre also included a process of producing its own clichés. But seeing these films as a series of black movement-images that challenged white common sense, they can be seen as successful. Drug trading, prostitution, and informal forms of labor and exchange as part of the nightlife would challenge classic notions of working 9 to 5, and women and cars would challenge stereotypes of white heteronormative symbols of success. While these characters could be criticized from a classic feminist perspective, Keeling provides a queer reading of them. Just as the word queer once was used to subjugate, hurt, and offend homosexuals, the term black was connected to the sexualization of racism and making the male macho and female prostitute negative stereotypes. Therefore it is at this intersection where black queerness would arise and become, as is shown in the early Blaxploitation films, a point of resistance. As Keeling comments:

> ...blaxploitation films are "queer," if we can understand "queer" to mark an antinormative positioning with regard to sexuality. Relying upon the affective labor of a young, urban, and black audience to valorize its depictions of pimps, prostitutes, drug dealers, and the like, blaxploitation films disrupt gender ideals and sexual norms while simultaneously staging and seeking to quell some of the anxieties that attend such disruptions.[72]

71 Keeling takes the term from Gramsci to describe an image that, on the one hand, has the ability to form a common sense perception and can be recognised as such, like the *black with the gun*, while on the other hand, a common sense image has the limitation of becoming a stereotype or a cliché, as the *black with the gun* also demonstrates.
72 Keeling 107.

Theatrical poster for *Superfly*

*

Sweetback's upbringing in a commune of sexworkers and also his participation in their unusually queer looking shows, which included crossdressing and also himself engaging in sexual intercourse (thus making him a sexworker as well), is clearly antagonistic to the notion of a white heteronormative middle class.[73] Furthermore the trade in drugs and other forms of informal, sometimes sexual exchange has nothing to do with conventional labor and the reproduction of the nation state. A prostitute is not only a symbol of the suppressed female working class, but also maintains an antagonistic stance toward any idea of the nuclear family and thus, of reproduction. Moral or not, sexual interaction with a prostitute is structurally the opposite of a straight future finalized through producing the child as the continuation of the family. It is queer in the sense of being non-reproductive. As Roderick A. Ferguson has argued:

> Unmarried and sexually mobile, the prostitute was eccentric to the gendered and sexual ideals of normative (i.e., patriarchal) heterosexuality. That eccentricity denoted the pathologies, disorders, and degradations of an emerging civilization. Rather than embodying heteropatriarchal ideals, the prostitute was a figure of nonheteronormativity, excluded from the presumed security of heteropatriarchal boundaries.[74]

To continue the intersectional analysis of these films, now we encounter the feminist dimension of the genre. Soon women would become the center of attention and finally, black movie stars as well.

---

[73] In particular, Robert Reid-Pharr has done inspiring work about the *queerness* of *Sweetback*. See his chapter "Queer Sweetback" in *Once You Go Black: Desire, Choice and the Black American Intellectual* (New York: New York University Press, 2007) 146-168.
[74] Ferguson, *Aberrations* 9-10.

*

The best known among them is Pam Grier, an actress and symbol of female independence whose popularity would even grow bigger than that of any male star of Blaxploitation. Still an icon today, Grier became re-valorized in cult films like *Jackie Brown* (Quentin Tarantino, 1997) and the first lesbian mainstream-series *The L-Word* (Showtime, 2004-2009). Her performances in *Black Mama, White Mama* (Eddie Romero, 1973), *Coffy* (Jack Hills, 1973) and *Foxy Brown* (Jack Hills, 1974) became legendary echoes of a black power movement that also involved strong women – like Angela Davis, Kathleen Cleaver, or Assata Shakur. As Grier commented when asked about her performances back in the day: "My films in the seventies were about black pride. Foxy Brown and Coffy are strong women, who have a sense of righteous anger but still never lose their sense of femininity."[75]

Those films were released shortly after such classics as *Sweetback* (1970), *Shaft* (1971) and *Superfly* (1972), establishing a series of *women with guns*, which were not the least bit weaker than their male contemporaries. These women not only would affirm and represent a notion of black feminism, but also, along with the categories race and gender, influence a queer discussion about the notion of black sexuality. Grier was not only readable as a subject of desire for white and black men alike, but her non-normative, working class and non-housewife-like performance would also make her a fascinating subject of both desire and identification for lesbian women. The excess her persona creates obviously goes beyond the heteronormative framework. A subtle but obvious reference is given at the beginning

---

[75] Pam Grier, "Es Geht Nur Um Körper. Interview mit M. Stocker," *Süddeutsche Zeitung*, 19 Aug. 2006, http://www.sueddeutsche.de/kultur/385/306347/text/

*

of *Black Mama, White Mama* (1973). Pam Grier, of course depicted as a prostitute, is imprisoned together with a white anarchist (Margaret Markov). The whole story is a narrative of breaking out from jail and fighting for survival. While the social positions of a prostitute and an anarchist clearly reference female political narratives that go against the mainstream, their physical, homosocial connection is underlined by the handcuffs, which tie them together throughout the narrative.

Theatrical posters for Margaret Markov and Pam Grier in *Black Mama, White Mama* and Pam Grier as *Foxy Brown*.

*

The film reacts to these subversive, queer excesses by producing a process of normalization. Pam Grier's character seems to pose such a threat that its queer potential has to be controlled by the narrative. From this point of view it is no surprise that she won't engage in the sexual interest shown to her by a female prison guard. In *Foxy Brown* the tables are turned as well. Here she performs the classic *woman with a gun* as a secret agent who does undercover work as a sexworker to sabotage a prostitution ring.

A last example of women in Blaxploitation that is worth noting is Tamara Dobson as *Black Cleopatra* (Jack Starret, 1973). While Grier's characters usually needed the narrative to work their way up to becoming a respectable woman, Black Cleopatra already seems to have it all: the respect of whites and blacks, plus the skills of a super-hero. She is as femininely beautiful as she is powerful, a specialist in kung fu, drives the hottest cars around and is a special agent for the state. She is not lacking anything in comparison to male classic figures like James Bond. As if the Blaxploitation heroine has undergone a successful integration into American cinema, the perfection of Dobson's character is mindblowing. She has no problems dealing with her male colleagues, but is able to solve conflicts in the ghetto that white police officials are clearly not able to. She is also friendly with a black emancipatory organization and supports their struggle. The film ends with the funny image of a white cop surrounded by blacks pushing his fist in the air. It is as if she even managed to include white policeman in the black power struggle. From an intersectional perspective, however, Cleopatra Jones has nothing good to say about white feminism. Jones's main foe is a character called Mommy (Shelly Winters), an evil drugloard and, compared to Cleopatra Jones, a totally un-feminine lesbian that fits into any negative chauvinist stereotype about white feminism. Evil to both men and other women alike, badly dressed and unsensual, she embodies the cliché of the castrative bad mother. Obviously this leads to the consequence that she will be punished in the narrative and die. Here we can see how multi-faced interlocking constellations of power and identity can work together, but also against each other. Not only would Cleopatra Jones be so versatile as to defend herself through the art of kung fu. It might be that her name was inspired by *Black Belt Jones* (Robert Clouse, 1974), the first black kung fu hero in the Blaxploitation genre. Coined Black Fu, the cross-identificatory move that Blaxploitation heroes and heroines made was appropriating martial arts. This shows the influence of minoritarian action-heroes such as Bruce Lee and the identification with another minority in the US: Asians. Thus, the heroes of Blaxploitation would distinguish themselves from the classic *black with the gun*, who had already become a stereotype by the middle of the seventies. The higher art of kung fu thus symbolized a higher ethical identification for the black heroes and functioned as an alternative to the destructiveness of both black and white gangs, drugs, and gun violence. Furthermore the art of kung fu seemed less phallic than the use of the gun, therefore it might be no wonder that *Black Belt Jones* includes both male and female heroes.

*

Theatrical posters for *Cleopatra Jones* and *Black Belt Jones* (The black hero becoming Asian).

4.0 QuAre Theory and the Heterogeneity of Black Situativity

*

In E. Patrick Johnson's wonderful essay "Quare Studies, or (Almost) Everything I Know About Queer I Learned from my Grandmother" he remembers how his grandmother would, in her "thick, black, Southern dialect"[76] pronounce the word "queer" as quAre. One could argue that this sonar disruption subverts the sound and meaning of the now canonical term queer and relates it to the Southern black trajectory of post/slavery, while putting the "A" of the black in the center of queer. Johnson also underlines that what his grandmother means by quAre are characteristics that are already associated with the term queer: "On the one hand, my grandmother uses quare to denote something or someone who is odd, irregular, or slightly off kilter,"[77] while on the other hand it functions as an echo of the slavery-past and sounds like a slang version stemming from black vernacular cultures.

But the anecdote of Johnson's grandmother also shows the paradoxical relationship queers of color have to their post-slavery trajectory. While his grandmother is depicted as unfortunately homophobic and thereby neglecting part of her grandson's identity, Johnson also addresses how much he learned from her about racism, sexism, the trajectory of post-slavery and therefore: his own survival. Thus quAre is a contradictory term that cannot be reduced to a simple addition of supposedly analogous categories of race and sexuality.

---

76 E. Patrick Johnson, "'Quare' Studies, or (Almost) Everything I Know about Queer Studies I Learned from My Grandmother," *Black Queer Studies: A Critical Anthology*, ed. E. Patrick Johnson and Mae G. Henderson (Durham: Duke University Press, 2005) 126.
77 Ibid.

*

Still, quAre might function as a subtle but productive intervention into the predominantly white term queer. Even if not ideologically or intentionally racist, the unmarked whiteness of queer and its origins in white, western discourses has already provoked many discussions in queer of color contexts:

> ...there are gay, bisexual, lesbian and transgendered people of color who embrace "queer." In my experience, however, those who embrace the term represent a small minority. At the Black Queer Studies in the Millennium conference, for example, many of the attendees were disturbed by the organizers' choice of "queer" for the title of a conference on black sexuality. So ardent was their disapproval that it became subject of debate during one of the panels.[78]

An intersectional "Quare Theory," as Johnson writes, "not only speaks across identities, it articulates identities as well. QuAre offers a way to critique stable notions of identity, and at the same time, to locate racialized and class knowledges."[79] This also becomes clear when we look at further queer of color positionalities, for instance in the influential *Black Queer Studies* reader.[80] Furthermore, social theorist Cathy J. Cohen criticizes queer studies for ignoring the multifaceted implications that race and ethnicity have on subjects marked as colored:

---

[78] See footnote in Dwight A. McBride, *Why I Hate Abercrombie & Fitch: Essays On Race and Sexuality* (New York: NYU Press, 2005) 87.

[79] Johnson 127.

[80] E. Patrick Johnson and Mae G. Henderson, eds., *Black Queer Studies* (Durham: Duke University Press, 2005).

> Personally speaking, I do not consider myself a "queer" activist or, for that matter, a "queer" anything.... Like other lesbian, gay, bisexual or transgendered activists of color, I find the label "queer" fraught with unspoken assumptions which inhibit the radical political potential of this category.[81]

In this sense, Cohen, who identifies as a black lesbian, puts together a quAre constellation of identity politics that includes race and sexuality as well as class and gender. The title of the essay that was quoted is "Punks, Bulldaggers and Welfare Queens," and sums up different derogatory terms for black women that for her should be included in a black queer theory. The "welfare queen" signifies a black working class mother that embodies the negative stereotype of the bad, unemployed mother sitting at home with her children and getting too much welfare from the state – the racist projection of a prototypical parasite without any social function. As with the bulldagger, who embodies the non-heteronormative looking, working-class masculine black woman, it is not the category of homosexuality that makes her queer but the constellation of many, different racialized gender and class positions that make her excluded and a threat to the white, heteronormative agenda.

Here we can see that a dualistic approach concentrating on "just" sexuality would not be able to locate these subject positions. A quAre point of view demonstrates how interlocking markings of power are embodied in a hybrid way, mixing race and gender, sexuality and class. These multiple categories, for Cohen, also connote multiple

---

[81] Cathy J. Cohen, "Punks, Bulldaggers and Welfare Queens," *Black Queer Studies*, ed. E. Patrick Johnson and Mae G. Henderson (Durham: Duke University Press, 2005) 35.

*

coalitions. Instead of looking for a truly queer and (often, unmarked white) subject, her point is that women of color can't afford only to bond with one group and identity. She especially attacks simplified notions of monolithic understandings of heteronormativity, as different sorts of (for instance, colored) communities might be important to the concrete survival of subjects suffering under multiple forms of oppression: "Further, a queer politics that demonizes all heterosexuals discounts the relationships — especially those based on shared experiences of marginalization that exist between gays and straights, particularly in communities of color."[82]

She reminds us of how, for example, the idea of white supremacy[83] under and after slavery was based on a white, and therefore purified form of heterosexuality. Marriage between slaves was forbidden, and mixed marriages were stigmatized even in post-slavery times. Therefore quAre not only moves a different path than the unmarked white binary of heterosexual and homosexual, or, heteronormative and queer. As Johnson sums it up: "…the model of quare studies that I propose would not only critique the concept of 'race' as historically contingent and socially constructed/performed, it would also address the material effects of race in a white supremacist society."[84]

---

82 Cohen 34.
83 Cohen 38.
84 Johnson 135.

4.1 Homonationalism and Biopolitics

Johnson and Cohen make us aware of a non-hierarchical, intersectional, quAre approach that can take account of certain precarious subjects, which are underrepresented in hegemonic forms of gender theories. A deconstruction of the white homonormative subject is also at stake in the contemporary queer of color critique of homonationalism. Close to how the white queer theorist Lisa Duggan once used the term homonormativity to criticize queer inclusion and normalization through whiteness, consumption, military, and marriage,[85] the critical perspective of homonationalism looks at how certain bodies are included into the reproduction of the family and the state, while others are not. Roderick A. Ferguson has analyzed how most homosexual marriages are between white, mostly male homosexuals in the middle class. Those couples have less problems becoming a part of the normal and have access to a form of inclusion that many fragmented black families don't reach:

> In addition to ignoring the particular concerns and needs of people of color and the poor, marriage as the sign of normativity extends racial discourses that understand women of color who head single-parent homes as the antitheses of citizenship and normativity.[86]

---

[85] See, for instance, Lisa Duggan's "The New Homonormativity: The Sexual Politics of Neoliberalism," *Materializing Democracy: Toward a Revitalized Cultural Politics*, ed. Russ Castronovo and Dana D. Nelson (Durham: Duke University Press, 2002).

[86] Roderick A. Ferguson, "Rac-ing Homonormativity," *Black Queer Studies*, ed. E. Patrick Johnson and Mae G. Henderson (Durham: Duke University Press, 2005) 61.

*

Another interface of inclusion and assimilation is the military. In the military, queers had to submit to a silencing "Don't Ask Don't Tell" logic and make their homosexuality invisible. From a post-slavery perspective, the military is obviously not an innocent context. Even if classic slavery seems over, remembering this colonial project where hundreds of thousands of Africans were kidnapped, common imperial wars would also make blacks and queers alike suspicious of the function of the military with its paradoxical inclusion of queers through silencing them:

> As the nation-state loses coherence because of shifts in the U.S. economy, because of its need for a heterogeneous workforce, and because of the challenges to national authority in the wake of processes of globalization that have no respect for national boundaries, homonormative formations emerge to recuperate the national identity's coherence.... In this post-September 11th moment, the United States remilitarizes itself to assert hegemony over Arab and Muslim Nations.... The virtually normal and authentic gay helps situate the Muslim and the Arab within the colonial gaze of the state.... Abroad, this means endorsing the brutal disciplinary measures of the U.S. government. Domestically, this means supporting ... panoptic techniques of discipline against Arab and Muslim immigrants as well as Arab Americans.[87]

The possibly most elaborate queer critique about contemporary American imperialism and war has been developed by queer of color theorist Jasbir Puar. Her book *Terrorist Assemblages*:

87 Ferguson 63-64.

*

Homonationalism in Queer Times investigates the anti-Muslim turn after the terrorist attacks of 9/11.[88] Since these events, she argues, every Arab body is marked as Muslim and thereby as a potential threat and a symbol of death through being linked with the notion of the terrorist. Here it is the supposedly explosive Arab body that poses the danger to American public space. The consequences of this anti-Muslim paranoia were not only the wars in Iraq and Afghanistan, but also new forms of everyday racism and the intensification of racial profiling and surveillance. Thus, while white homosexual bodies experience new forms of inclusion, colored, especially Muslim bodies experience new forms of exclusion. As Foucault reminds us, it was in the eighteenth century that life itself became the center of control and regulation in the modern nation state: biopolitics. The governance of life invented, in this sense, the human itself as a species to be governed through different forms of what he called *dispositifs*. As Puar elaborates:

> Biopolitics, as Foucault explains, is the process by which humans become a species (and in fact, specimens) to join all other biological species. This becoming is also the process by which anthropomorphic frames of the human take force and are consolidated. A paradox occurs: the animalism of humans is taken up as a project of population construction, and humans join species. The (androcentric) human is thus rearticulated as an exceptional form of animality within an anthropomorphized category: "humanity."[89]

---

88 Addressing the anti-Muslim turn after 9/11 obviously doesn't make the terror-attacks of Al-Qaeda any better.
89 Tim Stüttgen and Jasbir K. Puar, "Ein Knotenpunkt von vielen. Interview mit der Queer-Theoretikerin Jasbir K. Puar zu Fragen des Posthumanismus," Springerin, 1/13 (2013), original transcript of the interview.

*

While biopolitics were established to discipline and control citizens in terms of birth and death rates, life length and health, the sexual *dispositif* in this context was especially concerned with the notion of the family and reproduction, and therefore: heteronormativity. While the nuclear family would symbolize health, reproduction, consumption, and thus a future of the national body, the homosexual was invented as a species signifying non-reproduction, or, in the connection between queerness and AIDS: death. This dualism has been turned around since 9/11, notes Puar. While some homosexuals have been somewhat included into neoliberalism and therefore into the reproduction of the nation state, Muslim bodies have been excluded and become the new marker of death through the ideological association of the colored/Arab/Muslim/fundamentalist/terrorist body[90].

90 However, one problem that has to be addressed with Puar is that unfortunately she doesn't investigate the ideologies of different terrorisms themselves. Especially jihadist terrorism identifies, one should at least note, with the deathly negativity of suicide-terror-act as an act for a higher, heavenly sake. While a lot of analysis in her book *Terrorist Assemblages* on new forms of Muslimophobic racism and homonationalist biopolitics is important, the title of her book somewhat suggests that the terrorist body would be somewhat queer – a notion that I find problematic. While she rightly criticizes new actions of inner-state racism and exterior wars, she forgets to also criticize jihadist terrorism itself, which seems like the most radicalized, problematic, and nihilistic actualization of Fanon's explosive body. Fanon's pathos-like image of pure, revolutionary violence here reaches its absolute limit, as a purely destructive act of negativity, mostly motivated by nationalist and religious-fundamentalist aspirations that are far from quAre or progressive in any sense of the word. It has to be noted that Fanon, in his work about the Algerian Revolution, doubted that it was worth joining the circle of terror and counter-terror, even if it was for the sake of freedom. Quoted in Udo Wolter, *Das obscure Subjekt der Begierde. Frantz Fanon und die Fallstricke des Subjects der Befreiung* (Münster: Unrast Verlag 2001) 79. However, the most popular parts of his work *The Wretched of the Earth* (New York: Grove Press, 2004), including the introduction by Sartre, became legendary for precisely this militarized and non-reflective nationalism that, for all its historical context and the rights of the suppressed to defend themselves, has to be criticized from a contemporary perspective as a limited and naive anti-imperialist strain. Its ultra-nationalist and not always emancipatory consequences were neither foreseen nor critiqued by Fanon. As we can see today and is both the case with some Arab but also some Afro-American nationalisms such as the Nation of Islam, even though they played some

*

As Foucault underlines in his less often mentioned writings on racism, especially in his lecture series *Society Must Be Defended*,[91] while sexual notions of health and reproduction are governed and regulated in terms of the *quantity* of the national body, racism has been concerned with the *quality* of the national body, both through the notion of the linking between kinship, blood, and citizenship and with it, the differentiation and hierarchization of different races as a caesura in the biological spectrum. As Foucault notes:

> What is in fact racism? It is primarily a way of introducing a break into the domain of life that is under power's control: The break between what must live and what must die. The appearance within the biological continuum of the human race of races, the distinction among races, the hierarchy of races, the fact that certain races are described as good and that others, in contrast, are described as inferior: all this is a way of fragmenting the field of the biological that power controls…. That is the first function of racism: To fragment, to create caesuras within the biological continuum addressed by biopower.[92]

So the biological caesuras differentiate between lives that are hailed as reproductive and thereby have to be *included into life* and lives that are hailed as unreproductive and thereby are *excluded from life*.

---

emancipatory role in the history of people of color, they were also often founded on sexism, homophobia, and also on anti-Semitism. That's why non-violent and diasporic notions such as the Black Atlantic and quAre interventions by Sun Ra play such an important role in their conceptualization, as we will see in the upcoming chapter. For a critical reading of Fanon's project, see Wolter, *Das obscure Subjekt*.

91 Michel Foucault, *Society Must Be Defended: Lectures at the Collège de France, 1975-1976*, ed. Mauro Bertani and Alessandro Fontana (New York: Picador, 2003).
92 Foucault 255.

*

These logics, Foucault notes, resonate with the logics of national wars in the sense of: "If you want to live, the other must die."[93] And these logics are included in biopolitical state politics as a biological relationship: The more the inferior and abnormal species diminish, the more healthy and pure the normalized species can proliferate. As Foucault makes clear:

> In the biopower system ... killing or the imperative to kill is acceptable only if it results ... in the elimination of the biological threat to and the improvement of the species or race.... Once the State functions in the biopower mode, racism alone can justify the murderous function of the State.... And if, conversely, a power of sovereignty ... wishes to work with the instruments, mechanisms and technology of normalization, it too must become racist. When I say "killing," I obviously do not mean simply murder as such, but also every form of indirect murder: the fact of exposing someone to death, increasing the risk of death for some people, or, quite simply, political death, expulsion, rejection, and so on.[94]

For Puar, the point is not only that these dynamics were actualized through the justification of both new exterior wars and interior racism, but also that these actions were justified by arguments of the formerly excluded, both feminist and queer. While the US military represents itself not only as a gender sensitive place because of the inclusion of women and (invisible) homosexuals, its imperial project is also trying to present itself as progressive since it would save oppressed women

---

93 Foucault 289.
94 Foucault 289-290.

*

from their fundamentalist husbands in sexually backward countries. Like the postcolonialist theorist Gayatri C. Spivak once noted, these logics function in the rhetorics of "white men saving brown women from brown men."[95]

Interestingly Ferguson and Puar don't leave it at an intersectional, dualist anti-white position. Instead they try to break up the intersectional net of categorial blocks and make us aware that even the most multiple forms of intersectionality cannot provide adequate abstractions from a much more hybrid and mixed-up worldly experience. For them, intersectional approaches in their presentist sense are somewhat analogous to new forms of both *inclusive* consumerist and *exclusivist* police-like character profiling and still present reality in a categorial, additive way. As Ferguson puts it, thinking worlds in categories, as racist sciences and laws also did, might in itself mirror the hegemonic approach of the presumably objective sciences: "To assume that categories conform to reality is to think with, instead of against, hegemony."[96] Therefore a radical queer of color position should open up to anti-identitarian politics. In his words, "intersections are necessarily messy, chaotic and heterodox. Why necessarily so? Because intersections are not about identity."[97] Puar also notes:

---

[95] Gayatri Chakravorty Spivak, "Can the Subaltern Speak?", *Marxism and the Interpretation of Culture*, ed. Cary Nelson & Lawrence Grossberg (Chicago: University of Illinois Press, 1988), 297. However, the point is not to decide now "against" white queers and for people of color, but the dynamic of homonationalism is especially worrying for people living in-between, such as women of color and queers of color.
[96] Ferguson 5.
[97] Ibid.

> Intersectionality demands the knowing, naming and thus stabilizing identity across space and time, generating narratives of progress that deny the fictive and performative of identification... As a tool for diversity management, and a mantra for liberal multiculturalism, intersectionality colludes with the disciplinary apparatus of the state.[98]

Therefore, she looks at queerness in the sense of disrupting this closed system:

> There is no entity, no identity, no subject to queer, rather queerness coming forth at us from all kinds of directions, screaming its defiance, suggesting a move from intersectionality to assemblage, an affective conglomeration that recognizes other contingencies of belonging ... that might not fall so easily into what is sometimes denoted as reactive community formations — identity politics — by control theorists.[99]

The notion of the control theorist lets us remember that forms of differentiated marking and profiling have existed for many years in nationalist spaces like in the army and the border police, but also in new neoliberal forms of representation and consumption, such as Facebook and Amazon. In a sense, these markers and codes function analogously to the realm of biopolitics, and with it, racist

---

[98] Puar, *Terrorist Assemblages* 127-128. However, she underlines in a footnote ten pages later that she doesn't want to disqualify the aims and strengths of intersectionality or propose a system which is totally outside of it: "This is not to disavow or minimize the important interventions that intersectional theorizing makes possible and continues to stage, or the feminist critical spaces that give rise to intersectional analysis." See Puar, *Terrorist Assemblages* 138.
[99] Puar, *Terrorist Assemblages* 211.

necropolitics. Thus, instead of breaking up identity into many more pieces and categories, and placing all forms of politics on the subject — an approach that might already be part of the strategies of the enemy — there should be new approaches in queer theory to grasp contemporary conflicts. Especially concepts of queer time offer an alternative to these models.

4.2 Queer Times

We have already seen that Blaxploitation cinema was political precisely in its relation to movement, with the *dangerous* black moving through public space and finally surviving, thus also opening a door to another black time, the future. A quAre temporality of Blaxploitation also exists in relation to labor. Instead of doing 9-to-5 jobs and coming back to the reproductive space of family, the anti-heroes of the genre work in non-reproductive, illegalized spaces of exchange like informal drug trade and sexwork, trades that mostly happen outside the temporally as well as spatially included working structures. Sometimes their life and work paths also intersect with another queer milieu, the bohemia, where they consume alcohol, have casual, non-reproductive sex and listen to jazz concerts. Judith Jack Halberstam has elaborated on these ideas in her book *In a Queer Time and Place*:[100]

> Queer uses of time and space develop, at least in part, in opposition to the institutions of family, heterosexuality, and reproduction. They also develop according to other logics of location, movement, and identification. If we try to think about

---

100 Judith Halberstam, *In a Queer Time and Place* (New York: New York University Press, 2005).

*

> queerness as an outcome of strange temporalities, imaginative life schedules, and eccentric economic practices, we detach queerness from sexual identity and come closer to understanding …that "homosexuality threatens people 'as a way of life' rather than as a way of having sex."[101]

In her book Halberstam tries to look for alternative spatial and temporal structures that are inhabited by queers, like, for instance, lesbian punk subcultures. These structures undermine the normative logics of the nation, labor, and capital. Also, instead of just dwelling in sexual identity politics, approaches to queer time can take account of more complex lives and relations than any intersectional profile could. Instead, notions of space and time not only question the idea of the authentic queer subject, but also take more complex dynamics of political society into account and are able to grasp collective and hybrid forms of activity.

From Judith Halberstam to Jasbir Puar, from Elizabeth Freeman[102] to Lee Edelman, time has become a noteworthy political concept in contemporary queer studies. For instance, Edelman entitled his last, much-discussed book *No Future*.[103] For him there is a normative dimension in the progressivist narrative of western civilization, where everything always gets better. When it comes to the nuclear family, the child symbolizes the perfect promise for the community that a better time will come. In this perspective, anal sex, for instance, a practice

---

101 Halberstam 1.
102 Elizabeth Freeman, *Time Binds: Queer Temporalities, Queer Histories* (Durham: Duke University Press. 2010).
103 Lee Edelman, *No Future: Queer Theory and the Death Drive* (Durham: Duke University Press, 2004).

⁂

that has been associated with gay perversion, non-reproductivity, and HIV,[104] stands in an antagonistic relation to these reproductive ideologies.

But while Edelman is mainly concerned with the gay white subject, queer of color theorist José Esteban Muñoz is still looking at the future as an important space for queer utopias. For him, queerness is a mode of the utopian per se, as it shows a never-ending dissatisfaction with the present of things. This position furthermore can be understood as a critique of intersectional presentism, since the intersectional analysis seeks to construct a presentist authenticity through the strict and totalizing hierarchy of the categories it uses. Instead Muñoz calls for a perspective of queer collectivity that does not sit so well with contemporary propositions of inclusion and appeasement. Clearly inspired by Jewish-German philosopher Ernst Bloch and his writings on hope and utopia,[105] Muñoz writes:

> Queerness is not yet here.... Put another way, we are not yet queer.... We have never been queer, yet queerness exists for us as an ideality that can be... The future is queerness's domain. Queerness is a structuring and educated mode of desiring that allows us to see and feel beyond the quagmire of the present.

---

104   Ibid. This doesn't mean unprotected bareback sex itself should be read as the new radical queer act, but rather makes us remember a time when homosexuals were marked as sick and dead bodies. To take Edelman at his word would make his theory look at least problematic, as the barebacking trend in gay cultures seems to nihilistically long for a gay negativity that got lost through its inclusion into life. Thus, while Edelman's polemic is radical and also theoretically ambitious, it seems unclear what kind of concrete political practice one should gain from his arguments.
105   A good start is Bloch's *Principle of Hope* trilogy. See Ernst Bloch, *The Principle of Hope*, Vol. 1 (Cambridge: MIT Press, 1986).

> The here and now is a prison house. We must strive, in the face of the here and now's totalizing rendering of reality, to think and feel a then and there.[106]

From this point of view, the "then and there" of queer utopia is neither escapist nor naive. Instead it performs a militant critical optimism against the nostalgia of the past and the limits of a now that always will fail to include all precarious subjects into the area of the human. "Queerness is that thing that lets us feel that this world is not enough, that indeed something is missing," writes Muñoz. "Queerness is essentially about the rejection of the here and now."[107]

As Muñoz lays it out, the domain of the queer is the ornamental, the aesthetic, and the performative. For him, the performative itself is "a doing towards the future."[108] This doing towards the future is what we will concentrate on in the upcoming chapters. The phenomenon of Afrofuturism as well as the communal practices of quAre free jazz performer and composer Sun Ra and his big band, the Arkestra, will be at the center of attention.

*

---

106 José Esteban Muñoz, *Cruising Utopia: The Then and There of Queer Futurity* (New York: New York University Press, 2009) 1.
107 Muñoz 1.
108 Muñoz 3.

Herman Poole Blount alias Sun Ra

5.0 Introducing: Sun Ra

*

The Afro-American free jazz composer and performer Sun Ra was born as Herman Poole Blount in Birmingham, Alabama on May 22, 1914. His biographer has described the city, where he was also buried on May 30, 1993, as the "perhaps most segregated city in the world."[109] In his lifetime Ra published more than 100 albums on important black avant-garde and free jazz record labels such as ESP and Impulse!, but also on his own independent label Saturn Records. Running his own independent label, independent also from the mainstream jazz record industry, which would feature many black musicians but still be made up of white label owners, was not the only extraordinary difference Ra would make when compared with the standard jazz players of his time. His unusually quAre costumes, his music, which he called *cosmic jazz*, and his complex philosophy of time make him an unusually rich example for contemporary queer of color readings. While most of his performative gestures were directed towards the future, his radical neglect of the racist, post-slavery present of his time would also connect him to gods and legends from the African past, most notably Tutankhamun. As John Szwed writes:

> He fell under Egypt's spell — became obsessed, some might say…. He believed that hieroglyphics, like the pyramids and monuments, held secrets, and were part of the system of Egyptian science…. He learned the power and the rank order of the gods, feeling special affinity for Ra of Heliopolis, the Egyptian sun god.[110]

---

109 See John Szwed interviewed in *Sun Ra – Brother from Another Planet*, dir. Don Letts, 2005. 2:30-2:45.
110 John Szwed, *Space Is the Place: The Life and Times of Sun Ra* (New York: Payback Press, 1997) 64-65.

*

Just as the ancient Egyptians developed a complex and secret science through their hieroglyphics, Ra would develop a whole black philosophy through his music. The self-made cover art of Sun Ra and his Arkestra already showed that their music would have a different approach than the usual coffeehouse jazz. The album *Sun Ra — and His Solar Arkestra Visits Planet Earth* (1956-58) showed the planet Saturn playing trombone next to a whole surreal landscape including pyramids, pianos but also abstract landscapes. A strange world of past and future images, a black science fiction that later would be called Afrofuturism.

After being a student and assistant of the big band leader Fletcher Henderson in the sixties, Ra would intensify his outer worldly presence through his costumes, which would make him look like a hybrid mix of god and despot, cyborg and alien. Also the music of his band would not stay in the realm of traditional jazz, where the notion of authenticity through analog instruments was still a high value. Instead Ra would include new electronic instruments like the Moog synthesizer and other keyboards, to produce the legendary cosmic jazz that had never been heard before.

Sun Ra's atonal, experimental sound would draw a mixed audience through his concerts and break the separationist dimension of black community music events. White audiences looking for a liberation of the mind, such as the hippies, would react very excitedly to his performances, which looked like psychedelic multi-media shows, but from a slightly different, black perspective. However, Sun Ra never used drugs and such substances were totally forbidden in his Arkestra. The Arkestra functioned like a commune with Ra as their disciplining

*

but not authoritarian leader, and for many of its members it became close to an alternative family community. In a sense the Arkestra was like Warhol's factory: a community that was like a family without its patriarchal dimension, but also a social factory that was extremely productive and that made costumes and record covers, music and performance all together as a collective unit.

Cover art: *Sun Ra & His Solar Arkestra Visits Planet Earth* (1966)

*

Ra would teach his students and fellows not only music and composition, but also lecture them in past and future histories of the black race.[111] He remade his life story into a queer, Afrofuturist myth. So even his birthday would become a part of his intergalactic narrative. In an interview he once claimed: "I arrived from a distant solar system and combusted in the Magic City – Birmingham, Alabama."[112] Another time he would even give his birthdate a notorious dimension: "I arrived on this planet on a very important day, been pinpointed by wise men, astrologers as a very important date.... A very controversial arrival, so that's the only reason I don't talk about it." One time he even did away with all the knowledge about his birthdate to make himself a citizen of the Earth for more than 1000 years. To Philip Schaap he said he had been living on Earth since "around 1055 or so. I didn't just arrive on the planet you know. I have been around for quite some time."[113]

Even his practice of self-naming would subvert the shadow of slavery that was still darkening his present. Since the slave owner would usually name his slave and give him a name in the Christian tradition to make it distinct from any African reference, Sun Ra would reconnect him with a different African past. The practice of black renaming was usually performed in the slave narratives, the first written documentations of post-slave history, where the former slave would give an account of his experiences and rename himself as

---

[111] Ra would even lecture at the respected university of Berkeley. See Sun Ra, the *Berkeley Lectures*, 1971.
[112] Interview quotes are from Robert M. Campbell, *From Sunny Bloundt to Sun Ra: The Birmingham and Chicago Years*. See http://hubcap.clemson.edu/~campber/sunra.html
[113] Schaap quoted in Graham Lock, *Blutopia: Visions of the Future and Revisions of the Past in the Work of Sun Ra, Duke Ellington, and Anthony Braxton* (Durham: Duke University Press, 1999) 47.

*

a symbol of independence, freedom, and agency.[114] Realism would be a major ingredient of the slave narrative. It was supposed to present "nothing exaggerated, nothing drawn from the imagination"[115] and was supposed to be "factual and truthful." Instead, Ra would go beyond the whole genre with the mythical, fictitious status of his narrative. As Lock explains:

> It is as if Sun Ra was deliberately reversing the formal conventions by which the slave narratives claimed to be documented truth, perhaps to signal that he was breaking the historical links (as an African American) with the fact and condition of slavery. Indeed, the points in which slave narratives end — with the acts of renaming — is the point at which Sun Ra's new narrative of mythic identity begins: a shift from history to mystery, past to future, time to space.[116]

Thus, for instance, the Arkestra would have more than 40 different names through its existence and even on the level of naming perform a never-ending futurity of blackness, a never-ending differentiation of new blacknesses to come. So the quAre fabulations of Ra's practice would always stay processual and could reinvent themselves for any coming day.

---

114 For an overview, a wide selection of slave narratives can be found in William L. Andrews and Henry Louis Gates, Jr., eds., *Slave Narratives* (New York: The Library of America, 2001).
115 Frederick Douglass, quoted in Andrews and Gates, *Slave Narratives*.
116 Lock 51.

*

5.1 Sun Ra and the Question of Homosexuality

Mostly kept as a secret, the outing of Sun Ra as gay would happen after his death. It seems he never committed such a form of (western) outing himself. Val Wilmer, for example, wrote in Sun Ra's obituary that was released in the British newspaper *The Independent* on the first of July, 1993: "Ra was gay himself, but the precise nature of his relationship to his associates has never been known outside that circle."[117] One can only imagine how important the unity of black liberation needed to be at this time, ignorant of supposedly minor identity markers such as sexuality. At the same time, it is not uncommon that the wave of black emancipation would also come with a strong sense of homophobia. As John Gill, who in his book *Queer Noises* highlights the homosexuality of black avant-garde jazz icons such as Sun Ra but also Cecil Taylor, notes: "Homosexuality, or rumor of sexuality, or any sense of 'gay pride' has a snowball's chance in hell in such an atmosphere, has been a sub rosa topic in jazz since its beginnings."[118]

Even John Szwed's major biography *Space Is the Place* never mentions Sun Ra's homosexuality (on more than 450 pages!). Instead Szwed presents Ra as *asexual*. As Ra is quoted in Szwed's book: "I have never been able to think of sex as a part of my life though I have tried to but just wasn't interested. Music to me is the only worthwhile thing in the world and I think of it as a full compensation for any handicaps I have."[119]

---

[117] See Val Wilmer, Obituary: Sun Ra, *The Independent* (London), 1 July 1993. http://www.independent.co.uk/news/people/obituary-sun-ra-1482175.html
[118] John Gill, *Queer Noises: Male and Female Homosexuality in Twentieth Century Music* (Minneapolis: University of Minnesota Press, 1995) 68-69.
[119] Quoted in Szwed 40.

*

John Gill interprets these comments as a kind of repression from his "real" identity and has no empathy for a musician, who, as I argue, might already perform an anti-normative quAreness that would challenge notions of gender, race, and the human alike, but not position himself in relation to his sexuality: "…it is saddening to think that Sun Ra could be out about so many things — not least his regal ancient Egyptian ancestors, and the fact he didn't come from his planet — but not about his sexual orientation.[120]

For this author, however, it is not about deciding for the one or the other. Neither do I want to ignore Ra's homosexuality, nor do I wish to make him gay after his death or even denounce him as a traitor that wouldn't out himself. I would prefer to link different anti-normative modes such as hidden homosexuality and performative asexuality to his singular, Ra'ish quAreness. This quAreness I want to connect to Fanon's nausea of the black man and to a quote concerning his own estrangement from his body. As Szwed writes:

> When he reached adolescence various psychological problems began to plague him, especially a severe hernia associated with problems of testicle development, cryptorchidism, an affliction whose name alone was a scourge. He concealed this as best he could, but it was a source of constant aggravation, a weakness that left him feeling that at any moment his internal organs might shift or drop, and forced him to be constantly wary; his body became a nuisance and an object of scrutiny to him, and left him fearful that others might find out and that he might be

---

[120] Gill 60.

*

> treated as a freak, like the carnival sideshow anomalies he saw every year at the Alabama State Fair. It was a secret affliction, which became an obsession and a curse, but yet also an emblem of his singularity.[121]

Next to these personal worries came Ra's insomnia. He wouldn't be able to sleep during the night and even in this sense lived in different times than his contemporaries. However, when it came to performing masculinity, his despotic alien drag could not be farther away from the performance of the *black macho* that was shaped in American racism but also appropriated in Blaxploitation cinema. One could also argue that performing the alien or the cyborg would reflect on the radical disruption blacks experienced from whites in the time of slavery. Many levels beyond the classic gender drag performed by drag queens and drag kings, the notion of alien drag would remind us of the radical dehumanization slaves went through in slavery the moment they were put onto the ship. There, black men and women were merely material of labor force, a dehumanized dimension where gender didn't primarily matter. Therefore, the distinction between man and woman such as existed in the white nuclear family, for instance through productive and reproductive forms of labor, would not be the main one defining black identity. In the next chapter, we will look beyond Ra and investigate a whole tradition of Afrofuturism, which challenged the racist present precisely through the decentralization of the human.

---

121 Szwed 10.

5.2 Afrofuturism: Genealogical Notes

> Calling planet Earth... Calling Planet Earth... I am a different kind of being... I inhabit a different kind of horizon.
>
> Sun Ra[122]

The concept of Afrofuturism was first elaborated by the text compilation *Flame Wars*[123] by cultural theorist Mark Dery, even though Mark Sinker and Greg Tate also get credit for inspiring the term.[124] Dery defines Afrofuturism as follows:

> Speculative fiction that treats African-American themes and addresses African-American concerns in the context of 20th century technoculture – and, more generally, African-American signification that appropriates images of technology and a prosthetically enhanced future – might, for want of a better term, be called Afrofuturism. The notion of Afrofuturism gives rise to a troubling antinomy: Can a community whose past has been deliberately rubbed out, and whose energies have subsequently been consumed by the search for legible traces of its history, imagine possible futures?[125]

---

122 See the legendary concert on a skyscraper in the documentary *A Joyful Noise*, 1980 A Joyful Noise. Robert Mugge, 1980.
123 Mark Dery, ed., *Flame Wars: The Discourse of Cyberculture* (Durham: Duke University Press, 1994) 180.
124 Eshun, one of the main theorists who helps to develop close readings on Afrofuturist music, clearly makes reference to Sinker and Tate here: Kodwo Eshun, *More Brilliant Than The Sun: Adventures in SonicFiction* (London: Quartet Books, 1998) 173-193.
125 Dery 180.

*

Like Blaxploitation, Afrofuturism in Dery's sense stems from minor genres, most notably science fiction, that have been excluded from the major cultural canon. For Dery, this also reflects the low social positions blacks held in American life in the seventies and eighties. But Dery also asks if the area of science and technology isn't already a hegemonic one, as it was also scientific progress represented through modern ships and weapons that made the Africans submit to be slaves. As he puts it, "…isn't the unreal estate of the future already owned by the technocrats, futurologists, streamliners and set-designers — white to a man — who have engineered our collective fantasies?"[126]
And later he would even emphasize that

> …especially perplexing in the light of the fact that African Americans, in a very real sense, are the descendants of alien abductees; they inhabit a sci-fi nightmare in which unseen but no less impassable force fields of intolerance frustrate their movements; official histories undo what has been done; and technology is too often brought to bear on black bodies…[127]

As we will see, it is precisely both the experience of alienation and of appropriation-like empowerment that made the speculative but highly imaginative genre of Afrofuturism such a powerful tool for new fantasies of black futures.

---

126 Dery 180.
127 Dery 180.

5.3 Afro-American to Alien, from Slaveship to Spaceship

> Rising up above what they call liberty and they call equality...
> Sun Ra[128]

One of the central images of Afrofuturism is the spaceship, whose meaning would not be easy to decipher if not through its flipside image, the slaveship. On the slaveship hundreds of thousands of slaves would be brought to America through the notorious "Middle Passage," the sea space between Africa and the Americas. Like many inventions that have made a brutal difference during slavery, the ship was also a symbol of modernity and globalism. However, white scholar Cesare Casarino already mentions the ambivalence of the ship and links it to the crisis of modernity: "If the nineteenth-century sea narrative produced the matrix of the crisis of modernity, such a matrix in these narratives was materialized above all as the space of the ship."[129]

The ship is also mentioned in Michel Foucault's writings on heterotopia. Unlike utopias, heterotopias are spaces where time and action function differently than in normalized reproduced structures of labor and institutions of capitalism. Places like the cemetery, the church, but also brothels and flea markets have their own functionality and include different traditions and rituals. And heterotopias also have a different temporality, or are sometimes only opened on special days or are open, like the brothel or the jazz club, during the night.

---

128 Quoted in Rollefson 107.
129 Cesare Casarino, *Modernity at Sea: Melville, Marx, Conrad in Crisis* (Minneapolis: University of Minnesota Press, 2002) 19.

*

As Foucault writes about the ship: "The ship is the heterotopia par excellence."[130]

While Casarino analyzes the ship in its ambivalent relation to newly emerging global dimensions of capitalism and Foucault categorizes it as a heterotopia, where days and nights function differently than on the mainland, black scholar Paul Gilroy categorizes it as a powerful motif of black tradition, which has its place in the works of black writers such as Frederick Douglass, Aimee Cesare, Marcus Garvey, George Padmore, and Langston Hughes.[131] He underscores:

> The image of the ship — a living, micro-cultural, micro-political system in motion — is especially important for historical and theoretical reasons…. Ships immediately focus attention on the middle passage, on the various projects for redemptive return to an African homeland, on the circulation of ideas and activists as well as the movement of key political and cultural artifacts: tracts, books, gramophone records, and choirs.[132]

Therefore the ship symbolizes a paradoxical interface between modernity and its regressions. As Gilroy continues:

---

[130] Michel Foucault (1986), "Of Other Spaces," *Diacritics*, No. 16 (1896): 27.
[131] Paul Gilroy, *Darker than Blue: On the Moral Economies of Black Atlantic Culture* (Cambridge: Belknap Press of Harvard University Press, 2011) 13.
[132] Gilroy 4.

*

Ships also refer us back ... to the half-remembered micro-politics of the slave trade and its relationship to both industrialisation and modernisation. As it were, getting on board promises a means to reconceptualise the orthodox relationship between modernity and what passes for its prehistory.[133]

Theatrical poster, *The Brother from Another Planet*

133 Gilroy 17.

*

For the slaves, after being kidnapped from their homeland, modern America must have been an alienating experience. This experience is thematized in John Sayles's *Brother from Another Planet* (1984) where a black alien called "Brother" (Joe Morton) arrives on Earth and experiences industrialized New York as an absurd backdrop for grotesque actions with no common use. The objects and people "Brother" interacts with even make his alienation worthwhile. Distinct from the humans, he is not even able to speak but stays completely mute throughout the narrative. Clearly not arriving at any point of integration, the aliens take him back. One wonders if this is not even to be interpreted as a kind of rescue, as Planet Earth seems to have nothing to offer him.

Black sound theorist Kodwo Eshun has emphasized how central the idea of alien abduction is for Afrofuturist visual discourses in his book *More Brilliant than the Sun*:

> And there's the key thing.... The idea of alien abduction, the idea of slavery as an alien abduction which means that we've all been living in an alien-nation since the 18th century.... The mutation of African male and female slaves in the 18th century into what became negro, and into the entire series of humans that were designed in America.... the key thing ... is that in America none of these humans were designated human.[134]

While the black alien in *Brother from Another Planet* stays alienated, which sometimes results in irony and humor, but not into progression or even emancipation, the future of Afrofuturism would represent

---

134 Eshun 192-193.

*

Afro-aliens that are actually able to interact with the technologies around them and invent new concepts. In one of his most successful albums, *Mothership Connection* (1974), George Clinton is shown jumping out of a spaceship in a playful and happy manner. As Clinton says in the documentary essay film *Last Angel of History* by black filmmaker John Akomfrah (1996): "The ... record had to find another place we hadn't perceived black people to be. And that was on a space ship. ...having come here from the planet Sirius." Clearly, the ship and its technologies are used in an affirmative way to produce another sound that would beam the listeners of *Mothership Connection* into another future.

What George Clinton was for funk music — a pioneer and innovator — and Sun Ra was for the jazz avant-garde, the Jamaican composer and producer Lee "Scratch" Perry was for reggae and dub music. Even today it is unclear if those three inventive figures knew about each other. Clinton, for instance, is quoted in *Last Angel of History* saying that he didn't know about Ra or Perry back in the day. Even if there are many more examples when it comes to Afrofuturist imagery, their legacy alone is more than extraordinary. This was also what John Corbett thought when he was researching black music utopias. As he writes:

*

> What is remarkable, uncanny perhaps, about the story of these three musicians ... is how they have independently developed such similar myths. Coming from different backgrounds, working in different musical genres, based in different parts of the music industry, making music for almost exclusively separate audiences, with divergent political and commercial concerns, Ra, Clinton, and Perry have nonetheless created three compatible personal mythologies.[135]

In *Return from Planet Dub* his whole sound is even situated on another planet. Perry returns to Earth, though, to enlighten the listeners with his non-human sounds. Of course, in the science fiction genre other planets are not only associated with being a threat to the human species, but also with technological and other knowledges that make this other species superior. Therefore aliens and their technologies function as a line of flight from the slave narrative and the racist present.

The necessity of breaking with history, and therefore an essentialist identity politics, had also already been mentioned in Fanon's *Black Skins, White Masks*, in the book's final epilogue:

> I am not a prisoner of History. I must not look for the meaning of destiny. I must constantly remind myself that the real leap consists of introducing invention into life. In the world I am heading for, I am endlessly creating myself.... But I have no right to put down my roots. I have not the right to admit the

---

[135] John Corbett, *Extended Play: Sounding Off from John Cage to Dr. Funkenstein* (Durham: Duke University Press, 1994) 11.

> slightest patch of being into my experience. I have not the right to become mired by the determinations of the past. I am not a slave to slavery that dehumanized my ancestors.[136]

But while these icons invented their personas in the sixties and seventies, today contemporary forms of hip-hop and soul also show traces of the Afrofuturist legacy. For example, the rapper Kool Keith has constructed the persona of Dr. Octagon, an alien gynecologist. The surgeon doctor crosses humans, aliens, and animals to produce new hybrid species and stems from the planet Jupiter. As "Black Elvis," another one of his many egos, he embodies none other than the singer who stole the blues from the black race and sold it to the major white record companies. Furthermore, Eshun makes clear that there is a whole trajectory of counter-appropriation of white sounds by black artists that has to be taken into account. See, for instance, the influence of Kraftwerk on Afro-American hip-hop and techno productions: "...listening to the whiteness of the synthesizer and using it because that sound would make them alien within America.... So it's the idea of white music being exotic to black American ears."[137] Today, sometimes even futurist black women and cyborgs are a part of the Afrofuturist kaleidoscope. Janelle Monae, like Sun Ra, performs a female cyborg character called Cindi Mayweather. Both nostalgic African references like the armor and the earrings connect with the identity of the futurist cyborg, close to the one Donna Haraway might have had in mind when she wrote her "Cyborg Manifesto."[138] While

---

136 Fanon 204-205.
137 Eshun 177-178.
138 See Donna Haraway, *Simians, Cyborgs and Women: The Reinvention of Nature* (New York: Routledge, 1992) 32.

one album cover makes reference to Fritz Lang's *Metropolis*, a film that, as white film theorist Siegfried Kracauer noted, foreshadowed German fascism,[139] the other one references the Afro-android again, including the biblical reference of the ark.

As we have seen, the Afrofuturist world is embodied by many different characters, which should be further investigated. Also their narratives are different and cannot be limited to a clear story like the mothership bringing its people back to Africa. On the contrary, next to new links to the past, visions of the future emerge that move beyond the framework of the human and the notion of national citizenship, as the whole dualism of inclusion and exclusion is called into question.

> This Afrofuturist subjectivity is then a tactical, contingent and embodied identity in that it recognizes the constructed nature of both the myth of the subhuman and the myth of the superhuman… By collapsing the past and the future onto the white supremacist present, these Afrofuturists simultaneously assert their new subjecthood and levy their dissent from the existing order.[140]

139 For the relationship between German expressionist cinema and the outbreak of Nazism, see Siegfried Kracauer's important standard work, *From Caligari to Hitler: A Psychological History of the German Film* (New York: Princeton University Press, 1947). Furthermore it should be noted that from a German perspective the notion of darkness or blackness has altogether different, negative connotations. Kracauer argued that the escapist fantasies of expressionism, which were often macabre and dark, foreshadowed the irrational desire for a new leader. Also the Nazis used black uniforms and so on. Thus, while the Afro-American fantasies of freedom can be read as liberatory here, even when they address images like *Metropolis*, as in Janelle Monae's album, from a German perspective these fantasies have an entirely different history. Obviously, this work is about the Afro-American dimension and use of these metaphors, not the German one.

140 J.Griffith Rollefson, "The 'Robot Voodoo Power' Thesis: Afrofuturism and Anti-Anti-Essentialism from Sun Ra to Kool Keith," *Black Music*

Cover art: George Clinton & Parliament, *Mothership Connection* (1974) and Lee "Scratch" Perry & Ari Up: *Return from Planet Dub* (2009)

*

Clearly, there is no perfect linear way back or even forward for blackness, but many paradoxically linked particles of a re-actualized past and a highly inventive future that might have found its home much more in the sense of a diaspora that is beyond and in between nations and times.

Kool Keith's cover art: *Dr. Octagon: Dr. Octagonecologyst* (1997) and *Black Elvis / Lost in Space* (1999)

Research Journal, Vol. 28, No. 1, Spring (2008): 89-90.

Janelle Monae's cover art: *Metropolis* (2008) and *Arch Android* (2010)

5.4 Beyond Black Nationalism: The Black Atlantic

The Black Atlantic in both its geographical as well as ethical implications poses a radical questioning of the nation – including the various currents of black nationalism. At the same time it stays a space of resonance for what happened on the many ships sailing through the Middle Passage. Therefore the Black Atlantic is both bound to an exilic past and to a diasporic present and future that goes beyond the lack of a lost home. As a system that includes historical, cultural, linguistic, and political communication whose roots lie in the enslavement and deportation of Africans,[141] the Black Atlantic is both a historical as well a virtual space that addresses historical forms of loss (like the loss of the homeland) as well as new, hybrid forms of belonging that see neither the way back to Africa nor any simplified black essentialism as the final goal.[142] For Gilroy, the age of post-slavery therefore gave birth to a new form of black culture, a form that precisely wouldn't rely on the essentialist notions of black liberation movements such as Negritude. The Black Atlantic is not held together through essence, religion or tradition. On the contrary, it connects the fact of ungroundedness and uses it for a progressive perspective of diaspora. As Gilroy elaborates:

---

141 See Gilroy 13.
142 A noteworthy addition to queer discourses on the Black Atlantic is Omise'eke Natasha Tinsley's "Black Atlantic, Queer Atlantic: Queer Imaginings of the Middle Passage," *GLQ: A Journal of Lesbian and Gay Studies* 14.2-3 (2008). It furthermore criticizes Gilroy's work for not addressing the real physical experiences of the captivated in the Middle Passage. This includes both the incredible amount of violence but also modes of sexual interaction and forms of resistant coalition by the slaves. Notable is also her definition of the *Queer Atlantic*: "Queer in the sense of marking disruption to the violence of normative order and powerfully so: connecting in ways that commodified flesh was never supposed to, loving your own kind when your kind was supposed to cease to exist, forging interpersonal connections that counteract imperial desires for Africans' living death." See Tinsley 199.

*

Diaspora is a useful concept because it specifies the pluralization and non-identity of the black identities without celebrating either prematurely. It raises the possibilities of sameness, but it is a sameness that cannot be taken for granted. Identity must be demonstrated in relation to the alternative possibility of differentiation, because the diaspora logic enforces a sense of temporality and spatiality that underscores the fact that we are not what we were.[143]

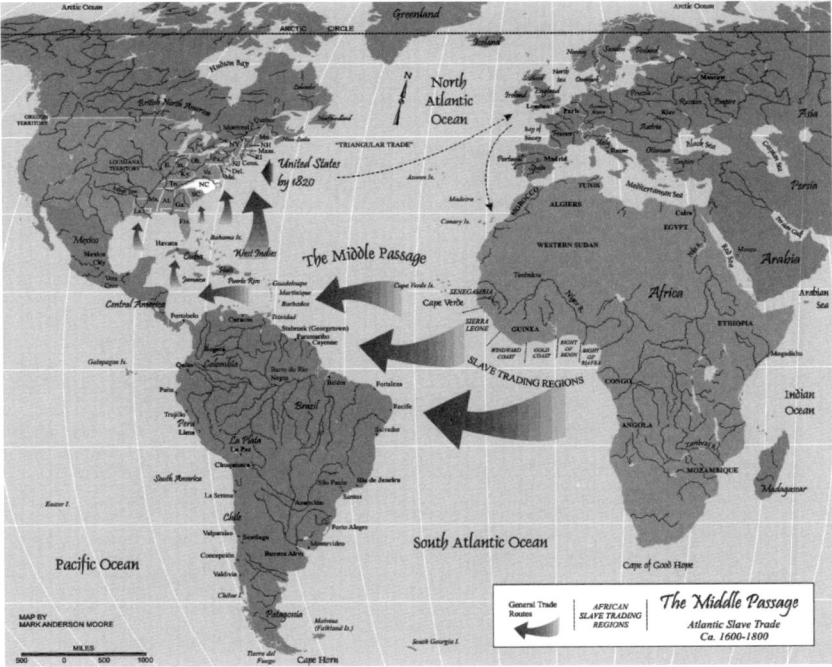

The Middle Passage of the slavetrade, a space that would become the hybrid, post-national diaspora of the Black Atlantic

---

143   Paul Gilroy, quoted in Sergio Costa, *Vom Nordatlantik zum Black Atlantic* (Bielefeld: Transcript Verlag, 2007) 128-129.

*

A major inspiration for Gilroy was the story of W.E.B. Du Bois (1868-1963), a black author who not only wrote the pioneering work *The Souls of Black Folk* (1903), but also had a scholarship as a student that would allow him to travel through Europe. For Du Bois it was clear that there was no white-versus-black cultural battle of purity to be fought. Instead, he took from European culture what he found interesting and useful for the idea of a black liberatory enlightenment. Du Bois defined three phases of black emancipation that would also play a role for Gilroy. First, concrete resistance to the institution of slavery, second, further forms of struggle for civil rights from an integrative humanist point of view, and third, the right for black-owned spaces, where black communities could produce their own statements and cultural articulations. This third phase, which after Gilroy is opened towards new forms of community and futures, is also closely associated with music:

> Though music plays a significant role in both of the earlier phases, the third can be defined by the project of liberating music from its status as a mere commodity and by the associated desire to use it to demonstrate the reconciliation of art and life, that is, by exploring its pursuit of artistic and even aesthetic experience not just as a form of compensation, paid as the price of an internal exile from modernity, but as the favoured vehicle for self-development.[144]

From this point of view, the historical and discursive worth of black music clearly goes beyond the limits of postmodern playfulness or of being trapped in the structure of the cultural industry. On the one

---

144 Gilroy 124.

*

hand it was especially music that the slaves would use to give account of oppression but also to articulate needs and utopias. One should remember that the slaves were not taught how to write and were excluded from education. So music became one primary space for black culture. Record shops, clubs, discos, and radio channels thus function as archives and future spaces for black cultural statements and resonances. Not even primarily bound through language, Afrofuturist visual and sonic politics could be called the radical music of the Black Atlantic, as it references both past traumas and futurist visions of new black subjectivities and practices. To contextualize the Black Atlantic even more, Gilroy relates them to Seyla Benhabib's notion of a politics of transfiguration, whose goals are not limited to forms of national inclusion. While those focus on the similarity of blacks and whites, the politics of transfiguration affirm the difference of blackness and cannot be translated easily into a language of the institutional state apparatuses. Interestingly, it is here that Gilroy also meets Muñoz, who underscored that a queer perspective that opens up to the future is connected to the aesthetic and the performative:

> This emphasizes the emergence of qualitatively new desires, social relations, and modes of association within the racial community of interpretation and resistance *and* between that group and its erstwhile oppressors.... The politics of transfiguration strives in pursuit of the sublime, struggling to repeat the unrepeatable, to present the unpresentable. Its rather different hermeneutic focus pushes towards the mimetic, dramatic, and performative.[145]

---

145 Gilroy 37-38.

In the next chapter, after analyzing both Afrofuturism and the Black Atlantic as contextual and genealogical backdrops, we will look more closely at the work of Sun Ra, especially by looking at the narrative of *Space Is the Place* (John Coney, 1974), and the politics of sound. As Gilroy states, these two formats have been particularly important for counter-constructions of the African diasporic self:

> Both storytelling and music-making contributed to an alternative public sphere, and this in turn provided the context in which particular styles of autobiographical self-dramatisation and public self-construction have been formed and circulated as an integral component of insubordinate racial countercultures.[146]

A closer look at the work of Sun Ra will help us understand how an Afrofuturist politics of transfiguration goes beyond and quAres the black common sense of the Black Panthers and the black movement-image of Blaxploitation. As we will see, Sun Ra's performative, visual but also sonic politics also pose an alternative to the *black with the gun* and invents a speculation of black futury that undoes limited notions of emancipatory struggle. Now, not only will the notion of another black futury become concrete, but also the concept of a new step in black cinema, which I, further deepening the dialogue between Fanon and Deleuze, will call the black time-image.

*

---

146   Gilroy 200.

6.0 Space Is the Place and the Black Time-Image

*

If we want to move from the black movement-image to the black time-image, we have to understand the paradigm that, for Deleuze, profoundly changed cinema. As already mentioned, the black movement-image as represented by Blaxploitation is a direct connection between physical action on screen and the montage of these movements into a narrative mediated through the main character, which works by recognizing already memorized structures or clichés. This interface is mirrored by the viewer's identification and produces a linear time in a closed world whose origin lies in the movements of action and montage described.

This closed world of main character-movement-montage-identification-linear narration is disrupted through the notion of the time-image. As Deleuze notes, the senso-motoric relation between the film world and the main character is loosened and brought to a halt precisely because something happens that goes beyond what the body and mind already know and remember. The point for Deleuze is that where movement stops, thought emerges. As Keeling explains: "For Deleuze, the time-image reveals a 'purely optical and sound situation,' thereby providing an opportunity for a sensory perception wrenched from habituated motor response to create a new perception."[147]

A new perception makes the viewer think something new, this is Deleuze's basic point. Moments of disorientation, dislocation, shock, and crisis make the movement-image tremble. At the moment when the protagonist — and the viewers with him — lose the dynamic connection to movement, outer events and new sensations intervene into the narrative, sometimes without any clear function, but also as

---

147   Keeling 15.

*

dreams and fantasies. In this moment the main character himself becomes a viewer, having to deal with the upcoming images and the appearance of another time and therefore, with thinking (of the new). One of the early examples of the time-image that Deleuze mentions are the films of Italian neo-realism.[148] Not surprisingly, neo-realism was not just another cinema tradition, but would emerge out of the dramatic European experience of the Second World War. Furthermore it would involve non-professional actors and use smaller, easier to carry cameras, which made it possible to shoot on the streets and in the real world, giving neo-realism a naturalist, nearly documentary quality. However, since for Deleuze all cinema is similarly mechanical, it was not any kind of realism that made him interested in the temporal qualities of neo-realism, but how new forms of time emerged that brought the movement-image into crisis. Here it might be useful to quote more than a bit from what Deleuze has to say about neo-realism and its relation to the time-image:

> What defines neo-realism is this build-up of purely optical situations (and sound ones...), which are fundamentally distinct from the sensory-motor situations of the action-image.... It may be objected that the viewer has always found himself... in front of optical and sound-images, and nothing more.... What the viewer perceived therefore was a sensory-motor image in which he took greater or lesser identification with the characters.... But it is now that the identification is actually inverted: the character has become a kind of viewer.... He is prey to a vision, pursued by it or pursuing it, rather than engaged in an action.[149]

---

148 Deleuze, *Cinema I*, 11-26 and 64-68.
149 Gilles Deleuze, *Cinema II: The Time-Image* (London: Athlone Press, 1989), 2-3.

*

Deleuze continues a bit later:

> In neo-realism, the sensory-motor connections are now valid only by virtue of the upsets that affect, loosen, unbalance, or uncouple them: the crisis of the action-image…. There is a new breed of signs, opsigns and sonsigns. And clearly these new signs refer to very varied images… subjective images, memories of childhood, sound and visual dreams or fantasies.[150]

In *Germany Year Zero* (by Roberto Rosselini), produced in 1948 and thus only a few years after the end of the Second World War, and which forms the final part of director Rosselini's war trilogy, the main character is Edmund Kohler (Edmund Moeschke), a boy who trembles disorientedly through his home city, the destroyed Berlin. His shocked awe when he looks at the bombed houses becomes part of the narrative. In a way, the character becomes a viewer who witnesses the impossibility of going back to a functional, innocent Berlin. His movements being in crisis, the film gives space for reflection on something that might be bigger than can be explained by any single character. At a climax of the crisis of his movements, the boy falls from one of the buildings and dies.

When it comes to formal notions of cinema, montage as the main quality of the movement-image has to give up its sovereignty to single long camera shots that articulate their own time, shots that may even be privileged above the notion of story or main character. As Tom Conley summarizes:

---

150 Deleuze, *Cinema II* 3.

> The time-image is what tends to govern cinema from the end of World War II until the present.... Seen less as matter than felt as pure duration, time-images relate a change in the configuration of the world.... They tend not to favour narrative or beg the spectator to identify with their content.... in the time-image, perception becomes a 'perception of perception,' offering a shift of emphasis that is witnessed in the image itself rather than the linkages between images.[151]

It is breath-taking, funny and surprising how John Coney's film *Space Is the Place* intervenes concretely into the linear Blaxploitation narrative and confronts it, through Sun Ra's spaceship landing on Earth, precisely in the America of the ongoing civil rights movement. If neo-realism represented a cinema dealing with the crisis of modernity after the Second World War, one is temped to ask if *Space Is the Place* indirectly deals with a similarly intense crisis of modernity: the legacy of slavery. Already during the exposition, the film presents a clip from another world. Before the audience is even introduced to some form of earthly narrative we follow Sun Ra walking through a spaced-out surrealism that seems to represent a peaceful harmony of nature, but also non-human figures who could be spirits or ghosts. They have no faces but mirrors where the heads should be, or plants with grown-out yellow hands. It seems that the film wants to situate Ra directly on another planet and in a non-human fantasy. While Ra walks through this fascinating landscape, wearing Egyptian symbols and headdresses, a strange music appears that could be none other than that of Ra's Arkestra, mixing jazz trumpets with fragmentary

---

[151] Tom Conley, "Time-Image," *The Deleuze Dictionary*, ed. Adrian Parr (Edinburgh: Edinburgh University Press, 2010) 280-281.

*

percussions. Then Ra starts talking: "The music is different here. The vibrations are different. Not like planet Earth. Planet Earth sounds of guns, anger, frustration. There was no one to talk to on planet Earth."

In this sense we are not just visiting some other world, but a world that is clearly presented as an alternative to Earth, where a messianic entity like Ra has "no one to talk to" and the atmosphere is diffused by "guns, anger, frustration." This outer perspective Ra offers us will not only challenge the doing of the black common sense as it was laid out by the Blaxploitation machos, it furthermore presents Earth only as one planet of many, shaped by white views, with blackness stemming from another world, a world that seems to be not shaped by events like slavery and not determined by white oppression.

At a closer look, one could argue that there are three different qualities of black time-images in the film. First, pure time crystals from another world, such as the opening scene, second, documentary footage of the Arkestra playing, delivering a different sonic world that seems to break into the narrative and is never introduced within it. And third, interfaces between movement-images and time-images, where the other temporality Ra represents directly intervenes into the narrative and becomes part of it. These are the moments when two genres also meet. The Blaxploitation genre collides with the Afrofuturist science fiction genre. An example of how Sun Ra not only breaks up the narrative structure of the film through other time-images, but directly challenges the narrative while still becoming a part of it, is the scene of Sonny Ray, Ra's character-double that exists in the worldly world of Chicago, where he works as a piano player.

Ra in the world he calls Alter-Destiny: Film still from *Space Is the Place*

*

6.1 The Subversion of the Black Entertainer

Earthly narration begins in the year 1943, as a subtitle informs us. After being introduced as an outer worldly entity, now Ra alias Sonny Ray is represented as an Earthling who works in an exotic dance club. It would be fair to note that this scene makes reference to Sun Ra's early years as a piano player, but also to jazz as a banal job, used for cheap entertainment and erotic dance soundtracks instead of for black emancipatory purposes. How limited the artistic freedom of Sonny Ray is can be seen in the intervention of the black pimp, who has just entered the club followed by two women worshipping him. Ray is just playing the piano during a break in the dance show, when the black pimp denounces his playing as boring and makes the boss of the club change the music and get the exotic dancers to reappear on stage. To underline his phallic presence, no gun is included in the scene, but a big cigar, which he passionately smokes. But the scene is also notable for showing the function of black entertainers in a predominantly white America. While being excluded from many jobs, they could make it as performers, sport stars, musicians, and entertainers, which were dependent on white recognition. As post-slavery theorists such as Saidiya Hartman have noted, black entertainers have an ideological function in slavery and post-slavery societies, as they performed their supposed symbolic freedom and potential happiness that would show no trace of the conditions they were enslaved under. So in the context of black entertainment, as Hartman argues, there existed a very ambivalent space between submission and agency. As Hartman elaborates:

*

> If through performance the enslaved "asserted their humanity," it is no less true that performance articulated their troubled relation to the category "human," if only because no absolute line could be drawn between the pleasant path of slave management and the collective articulation of needs, solidarity and possibility. While the pleasures afforded within the confines of slavery were vulnerable to... a critique of debased amusement and reactionary diversions, they also provided the occasion for small-scale assaults against slavery.... Thus, in this regard, it is impossible to separate the use of pleasure as a technique of discipline from pleasure as a figuration of social transformation.[152]

We don't know if Sonny Ray's reaction is mainly addressed to the black pimp or the white framework he has to do his work in, but soon his piano playing becomes anti-melodic, taking the structure of sound away that gave the exotic dancers' movements its harmony. And he doesn't leave it at that. After less than a minute the piano starts to burn as if the noise had lit a fire on the sensitive machinery. While the smoke fills the room like in a disaster film, glasses start to explode and the guests leave the club in panic. It seems like the outer-galactic sound of Sonny Ray's piano has changed the whole action of the film. The pimp, one of the few who was not scared enough to leave the club, is not happy about Ray's interruption of things. He asks Ray to play a card game with him to solve the conflict. His role as Ra's antagonist is highlighted by his title – the overseer. As the webpage Culture-Court comments:

---

152 Saidiya V. Hartman, *Scenes of Subjection: Terror, Slavery, and Self-Making in Nineteenth-Century America* (Oxford: Oxford University Press, 1997), 78.

*

> This is the Overseer. "If he sees something he wants, he gets it." His name suggests the slavery-era supervisor who takes care of business for white folks while his style reflects the stereotype of the big-shot ghetto operator in films like *Superfly*, the Mack who runs the rackets, shifts the drugs and pimps the girls.... If you want to put a neo-Gnostic gloss on it, the Overseer is the Archon who keeps the people enslaved in their sensual addictions; while Ra is the Divine Spark of the Pleroma who strives to lift them to a higher plane.[153]

The overseer not only resembles the obvious clichés of the Blaxploitation macho, but also shows what is left of the former anti-hero after he himself became black common sense. He has no relation any more to any anti-hero fighting police oppression or any state power, all he cares about is sex, money, and power, including violence against women. This critique of black masculinity and inner-community violence was very relevant for Sun Ra. It is noted that he pressured for the film to be edited into a 20-minute shorter version because he could not accept the heterosexist scenes that were part of *Space Is the Place*.[154] A longer version of the film would only be distributed after Ra's death in 1993.

But not only do scenes of violence against sexworkers show how a once potentially revolutionary black masculinity became part of the hegemony. The stereotypes of sexist men of color, whose value in life could be measured through women, guns, money, and fancy cars, continues in contemporary gangster-rap videos. Amongst others,

---

153 See: http://www.culturecourt.com/Br.Paul/media/SpaceisthePlace.htm
154 See: http://en.wikipedia.org/wiki/Space_Is_the_Place

*

Paul Gilroy has critically reflected on the hype around the car as a symbol of status.[155]

Black feminists like Michelle Wallace have analyzed how the symbolic castration of slavery, where more than once the white slave owners became the fathers of black women and black men had no possibility of claiming fatherhood and defending the family community and home, created the *black macho* as a counter-reaction.[156] Furthermore, in the shadow of the brutal position that was inhabited by the KKK in *Birth of a Nation* and that would later continue in the role of the police, the *black macho* could be understood as the internalized answer of the black violent militant. Even today, this constellation of black patriarchal masculinity is read as black authenticity. In contemporary rap, for instance, a masculine performativity that relates itself to the urban, the street, gangs, and violence is supposed to "keep it real." As E. Patrick Johnson notes:

> ...black authenticity has increasingly become linked to masculinity in its most patriarchal significations. That this particular brand of masculinity epitomizes the imperialism of heterosexism, sexism and homophobia, therefore, is not surprising.[157]

---

155 Gilroy 5-54.
156 Michelle Wallace, *Black Macho and the Myth of the Superwoman* (London: Verso, 1990) 20-21.
157 E. Patrick Johnson, *Appropriating Blackness: Performance and the Politics of Authenticity* (Durham: Duke University Press, 2003) 48.

*

Sun Ra's performativity poses a rare alternative to these notions of black authenticity. The overseer is depicted in the classic fancy suit and always surrounded by sexualized women, not only his big cigars symbolize potency. The radically quAre alien drag of Sun Ra on the other hand clearly undermines the clichés of hegemonic models of white and black masculinities.

6.2 Duel with the Overseer: Challenging the Black Macho

Therefore it is no surprise that in the narrative of *Space Is the Place* Ra is concretely positioned as the opponent to the black pimp. In another intervention of the black time-image, the worldly reality of the club is interrupted by a surreal scene in the desert, where Ra and the Overseer are sitting at a table and playing a mystical card game against each other, the goal of which is nothing less than the question of which direction the black future will take. It might be no surprise that Ra in this duel doesn't resemble any contemporary idea of the human. On the one hand, slavery dehumanized blacks much beyond a categorical distinction of gender or sexual orientation; on the other hand, it seems, from Ra's point of view, mimicking the human might end in reduced and regressive personifications of it, as the stereotype of the black pimp clearly demonstrates.

Duel with the Overseer: Film stills, *Space Is the Place*

*

The first round of the mystical card game starts with the question of mobility. While the Overseer draws a card with the notorious fancy car, as known from Blaxploitation narratives, Sun Ra draws a card with a spaceship. Soon he will land on planet Earth with it. While a group of curious humans awaits it along with the press, the ship arrives and opens its doors. Following their leader Sun Ra, a group of black creatures set their feet on planet Earth, mixing unusual clothes, which look both space-like and African.

Interestingly the spaceship seems to be driven by sound. In another scene we can see Sun Ra playing keyboards inside the ship, as if his improvisatory sound practice were the central way of navigating it. In this sense, the non-signifying practice of noisy free jazz improvisation precedes any form of language and visual representation or even becomes the practice of producing them. As Ra noted in the beginning of the film, speaking from the so-called Alter-Destiny, an alternative non-Earthly reality: "Teleport the whole planet here through: music."

The arrival of the spaceship: Film stills, *Space Is the Place*

*

While the long history of blues and jazz was not only connected to (also visual) narratives of black suffering and slave songs, and represented another form of black authenticity through the notion of the traditional instrument and the analog, the space sounds of Sun Ra's Arkestra clearly broke with the tradition — as if the slave songs were not the real songs of the black community. Ra was known to experiment with synthesizers and electronic effects long before it was fashionable in commercial jazz. Mixed with both classic instruments but also remakes of traditional African sound sources, the sound of Sun Ra's interplanetary Arkestra was extremely hybrid and went beyond any ideal of a black sonic tradition.[158] As Paul Gilroy notes, hybridity is also an essential element of the sonic culture of the Black Atlantic. He argues:

> My point here is that the unashamedly hybrid character of these black Atlantic cultures continually confounds any simplistic (essentialist or anti-essentialist) understanding of the relationship between racial identity and racial non-identity, between folk cultural authenticity and pop cultural betrayal … arguments are still made about the relationship between authentic jazz and "fusion" styles supposedly corroded by the illegitimate amalgamation of rock influences or the struggle between real instruments and digital emulators.[159]

[158] Still, one should note that, unlike white avant-gardes, which only address the new and the break with history, black free jazz resonates with both past and future. Stylistically different but symmetrically in its double-move, the Art Ensemble of Chicago for example used both traditional instruments and masks addressing Africa next to new sound sources and performativities.

[159] Gilroy 99.

*

Here we can see how the notion of black authenticity is not limited to representation, but also an issue regarding the politics of sound which is radically subverted by Sun Ra. In an important intervention with his book *More Brilliant than the Sun*, the Afro-British music critic Kodwo Eshun has produced an inspiring genealogy of anti-authentic black sound politics. Eshun argues that phenomena like sonic Afrofuturism not only should be understood in using anti-traditional instruments and producing new posthumanist interfaces between blackness and technology in genres such as Detroit house music, but also provoke a new form of journalistic reflection. Instead of endlessly repeating narratives of tradition, black suffering and the authenticity of the street and the ghettos — including interpreting everything with regard to the biography of the artists — Afrofuturism and similar phenomena clearly defamiliarize the notion of any authentic location:

> Rejecting today's ubiquitous emphasis on black sound's necessary ethical allegiance to the streets... The mayday signal of Black Atlantic Futurism is unrecognizability, as either Black or Music. Sonic Futurism doesn't locate you in tradition; instead it dislocates you from origins. It uproutes you...[160]

For Eshun, a critical perspective is necessary that takes the new sonic worlds of these musics seriously. In this sense the speculative sonic worlds themselves should be central to any critical writing about them, instead of being treated as gimmicks or as just another side factor of the same black music histories. Obviously, as *Space Is the Place* demonstrates, the outerworldly space-politics that Ra radically

[160] Eshun 3-4.

*

affirms are the key to understanding his contribution. Ra's future clearly is linked to an understanding of blackness that intentionally goes beyond anything already known or told. For him, any radical black position has to be articulated in relation to the future and the project of invention, including re-inventing blackness itself. Understanding the dehumanization of blacks in slavery as crucial and not being satisfied with any humanist myth of inclusion, he argues in one of his performances: "I am not a human being! I come from a different sort of horizon!... Some call me Mr. Ra. Some call me Mr. Ry. Some call me Mr. Mystery."[161]

6.3 QuAring the Community: Beyond Black Authenticity

It is no wonder that Sun Ra was considered a traitor by some people in a jazz community whose ideas were shaped by black nationalism. For instance, the jazz singer Betty Carter denounced Sun Ra's project simply as "bullshit" and commented that "he has got whitey going for it."[162] Even in *Space Is the Place* the question of Sun Ra's "realness" is reflected through the discussions of two black teenagers, if Sun Ra is "real" or a mere "sellout" that would use his idiosyncratic performances only for promotion and selling more records. These scenes reflect real discussions about the status of Sun Ra's political interventions. A symbolic anecdote about his ambivalent status in the black community is the story of the Arkestra's exclusion from a Black Panther owned house in Oakland, California. As Daniel Kreis writes:

---

161 See the famous skyscraper performance in the documentary *A Joyful Noise*. https://www.youtube.com/watch?v=UINN_bQzCPE or on Vimeo http://vimeo.com/3164191
162 Quoted in Ajay Heble, *Landing on the Wrong Note: Jazz, Dissonance and Critical Practice* (New York: Routledge, 2000) 120.

*

In 1971 avant-garde jazz musician Sun Ra was expelled from a house in Oakland, California owned by the Black Panther Party.... On the surface, the pairing of Sun Ra and the Black Panthers is a striking study in contrasts. The mystical Sun Ra, with his philosophies of time and space, flamboyant Egyptian and outer space costumes, and devotion to pursuing truth and beauty through music, must have seemed out-of-place to many residents of a city still watched over by leather-clad Panthers wielding a rhetoric and creating an iconography of revolutionary Marxist struggle as they engaged in direct neighborhood actions.[163]

In one of the central scenes of the film Sun Ra answers these doubts in his own way. Followed by mystical figures wearing the masks of Egyptian gods Horus and Anubis, he enters a black community center that is clearly representative of the community spaces that were created in many American cities since the nurturing commitment of black liberation. The posters on the wall also clearly reflect the ongoing struggle of black pride, representing influential figures like Eldrige Cleaver and Angela Davis, while one kid is depicted reading a book by LeRoi Jones. Black teenagers are shown singing, dancing, discussing, and playing pool; the beginning of the scene could even be part of a classic documentary reflecting black community work and experience in the late sixties or seventies.

---

163 Kreiss 57.

You are not real!
Sun Ra visiting the Black Community Centre.

*

Film still, *Space Is the Place*

*

This depiction of a classic black space of the times is obviously broken by Ra and his contemporaries, who provoke curiosity and laughter from the kids in the center. Politely, Ra starts up the encounter by introducing himself: "I am Sun Ra, ambassador from the intergalactic regions of the council of outer space." This makes the kids laugh more, asking their guest if he is "not a black hippie or something." Then they ask the central question of the discussion: "How do we know you're for real?" Ra answers:

> I am not real, I am just like you. You don't exist in this society. If you did, your people wouldn't be seeking equal rights. You're not real. If you were, you would have some status among the nations of the world. So we're both myths. I do not come to you as a reality, I come to you as the myth, because that's what black people are: myths. I came from a dream that the black man dreamed long ago. I am actually a present sent to you by your ancestors. I'm gonna be here until I pick up certain ones of you to take back with me.

In a provocative and, I would suggest, radically quAre manner, Ra asks the black kids to distance themselves from the domain of the human and its false promise of final inclusion and instead identify with the myths (of black people). The notion of myth here might not only reflect the many undocumented crimes in slavery that could only be accounted for through oral history and the slave narratives, but also the destruction of the link to Africa and its past. This lack, it seems, can only be countered by reactualizing the myths of a former motherland but also by creating new myths that are able to imagine a black temporality beyond both the traumatic past and the limited present.[164] Like the quAre Afrofuturist writer Samuel R. Delany once argued: "We need images of tomorrow, and our people need them more than most."[165] As Delany elaborates, the project of slavery has not only kidnapped and uprooted blacks, exploited their labor and enhanced their suffering, but also destroyed their history:

> The historical reason that we've been so impoverished in terms of future images is because ... as a people we were systematically forbidden any images of our past. I have no idea where, in Africa, my black ancestors came from because, when they reached the slave markets of New Orleans, records of such things were systematically destroyed. If they spoke their own languages, they were beaten or killed. The slave pens in which they were stored by lots were set up that no slave from the same area was allowed together. Children were regularly sold away from their parents. And every other effort conceivable was made to destroy all vestiges of what might endure as African social consciousness. When, indeed, we say that this country was founded on slavery, we must remember that we mean ... that it was founded on the systematic, conscientious, and massive destruction of African cultural remnants.[166]

---

164 Furthermore, one could argue that Sun Ra follows the logic of: If the advanced sciences of ancient Egypt had not been destroyed, the Egyptians would be the ones building spaceships now. In this sense, Ra is, as he says to the kids in the community center, a present from "your ancestors."
165 Delany interviewed in Dery 191.
166 Ibid.

*

While it was easy to follow that Ra would distance himself from the black authenticity represented by the *black macho*, his polemic rejection of contemporary black pride that is mainly focused on inclusion and human rights seems more difficult and complex. However, it is precisely this playful polemic (the scene is clearly not without humor!) that illustrates that the Afro-Americans, from both Ra's and Fanon's perspective, were basically the creation of whites as they were kidnapped from their land. Therefore, planet Earth is just one of many planets and no longer central in the universe. Thus, blacks not only need more representation on Earth, but a new world. As Sun Ra put it in the documentary *A Joyful Noise*: "All planet Earth produces is the dead bodies of humanity. That's its only creation."

Still, one should note the subtle differences between the two parties addressed in the film. While the pimp is clearly positioned as an opponent, the black youth in the community center are the people Sun Ra not only wants to address and convince of his messianism, but also the black power struggle is recognized through the various references of the pictures and writings represented in the scene. So even if there is a clear distinction between them, both projects share the goal of black emancipation through technology and the becoming of agents with the means of production. As Daniel Kreis summarizes:

*

Sun Ra and the Black Panthers stood in relation to the broader cultural and political movements of the post-World War II era that engaged in fundamentally performative projects to change consciousness in response to the psychological alienation caused by racism and the workings of a technocratic, capitalist society. At the same time, both appropriated technological artifacts and rhetoric and made them central to their identities in their respective projects of liberation.[167]

Therefore, while highlighting their differences, the Black Panthers and Sun Ra's Arkestra shouldn't be seen as fully antagonistic, even if Sun Ra's position can only be recognized by also recognizing its subversion of black common sense. However, for different purposes, a progressive critical race perspective should be able to support both positions for their different purposes and goals.

---

[167] Kreis.

6.4 Dixie Music: Bound to the Past?

After several rounds of a tight and sometimes hilarious battle about the future of the black race, Ra's final act in this duel is the organization of a concert with his Arkestra. While the audience is already impatiently waiting for the concert, Ra gets kidnapped — just like the slaves once were — by the FBI. The arrogant agents not only bind him to a chair and make him a captive, but also put a headphone on his head playing Dixieland music.

In the context of jazz, no other music could be described as so revisionist and clearly antagonistic to the sound of the Arkestra as Dixieland. "Dixie," or "I wish I was in Dixie" and "Dixie's Land" was the name of a popular song by the white minstrel and blackface performer Dan Emmett, who became a star in the US entertainment industry starting with his first performance in New York in 1859. In "Dixie," Emmet constructs the perspective of the black freeman who nostalgically longs to go back to the South, "in de land ob cotton." Obviously, this revisionist fantasy became popular amongst whites, as their longing to reinstall the conditions of slavery were nostalgically romanticized in these narratives. The message is obvious: Instead of affirming progress, liberation and a life in the liberal North, the blacks really missed their good old life in the good old South. The white researcher John Lock, for instance, mentions sarcastic situations where black workers were pressured to sing the song in front of their white bosses.[168] The song provided a name for a whole style of nostalgic folk music that can be clearly seen as the opposite to the emancipatory sounds of the black avant-garde. Lock writes:

168   Lock 72.

Bound by white history. Film stills, *Space is the Place*

*

> It continues to polarize opinion in the South, its performance at a range of occasions from state functions to football games still provoking protests from African Americans. "Dixie" can thus be seen as a song that whites have traditionally used to remind blacks of their "place", that is ... in the land of segregation and inferior status. The figure of the homesick Negro, wishing "to lib and die in Dixie", long persisted as a stereotype in American culture.... In the musical symbology of Space Is the Place, Dixie stands for the false history (his story) to be found in white misrepresentation of black life and black status.[169]

In the climax of the movie, Ra will finally be freed by two black kids who understand that Sun Ra is not a traitor, but is playing a relevant part in their cause. Consequentially, the traumatic loop of the past that the Dixie song was trying to reinstall, just like the endless repetition of colonial time that Fanon addressed, would be countered by the energetic performance of the Arkestra, that, even if it is noisy and bears some resemblances to the black explosivity mentioned by Fanon, is finally an affirmative and positive experience of collective joy and pleasure doing no physical harm.

---

169 Ibid.

*

6.5 The Present is Not Enough: Futures of the QuAre Performative

After the concert, which was notably attended by an excited black and white audience, Sun Ra beams a few of the black characters he had encountered during his visit on planet Earth onto the ship. In a sense, the music opens the space to another black future and intervenes successfully in the narrative of the same old stories both told by white revisionism and the stereotypes of Blaxploitation. Polemically, the last scenes of the film are staged as an Exodus from planet Earth. In this logic Sun Ra's proposition also reminds one of a radical interpretation of the flight from slavery and colonial time, an escape route from the Earthly present. It seems there is no real hope for Earth any more and therefore it explodes. In this sense, one could argue, not only the noise of the Arkestra actualizes the figure of the explosive black, but also more graphically, the final metaphor the film leaves us with is the end of Earthly life as we know it. Somehow the film itself seems to interpret this explosion as a metaphor on the irreparability of the crimes of humanity. While we see the spaceship leaving and pieces of the planet floating in all directions of the universe, a voice shouts as a final comment: "In a far out Place / In Space / We'll wait for you!" leaving the audience to decide for itself which way to go towards a better, and indeed, another future.

This leaves us with a final contradiction in Sun Ra, or, to put it more adequately, with multiple readings of a huge, complex, and sometimes contradictory oeuvre that can only partially be addressed here. While the performative and musical gestures of Sun Ra's work is clearly affirmative, posing an alternative to narrow, and partly violent forms of liberatory struggle, the radical critique of the Earthly present also

*

might be read as articulating a polemical, yet playful pessimism. As Gilroy notes, blacks were not only the passive audience of white supremacy and their new inventions, but also of their political conflicts like the Cold War. Here we can note another temporal dimension Sun Ra wanted to break out from: the totalizing dynamics of intense arms build-up as the ongoing preparation for a future potentially culminating into another world war. In a sense, Afro-Americans were concrete spectators of the worrying science fiction that was really happening on Earth: the real space race between the USA and the USSR in their trips to the moon, and the invention of the atomic bomb. These destructive dangers were clearly articulated in his song "Nuclear War" (1982), in which he cynically states: "Nuclear war / Is a bad motherfucker / If you push that button / Your ass gotta go!"[170]

What is crucial to understand here is that for people of color, white progress concretely looked like a science-fiction-like myth of white supremacy, which in the concrete sense of the word had the negative potential to destroy the planet. For Ra, this white present was not acceptable. This is also reminiscent of Muñoz's arguments about queer time: "Queerness is essentially about the rejection of a here and now and an insistence on a potentially or concrete possibility of another world."[171] From this point of view Ra's proposed alternative is not only post-national, but also post-Earthly and post-human. Thus, the quAre assemblage of Sun Ra's spaceship, which is just

---

[170] While Eshun clearly reads Ra as an antihumanist despot who has no respect for humanity, my reading would be that Sun Ra was primarily commenting on the destructive potentials of the white world's inventions, while posing an alternative through the finally positive, non-violent, and utopian proposition of his performances, records, and concerts. See Eshun 154-164.

[171] Muñoz 1.

one of many images, or the Arkestra and his vital sounds, decenters Earthly common sense and its straight white temporality. From this perspective, the black time-images of *Space Is the Place* can be read as indirectly but consequentially posing slavery as a paradigm that cannot be fully overcome without radically questioning the constitution of the human itself. This is not only supported by the Afro-alien performativity of the Arkestra and the funny, yet serious narrative of the film, but also found in the sonic politics of the music itself, which subverts the notion of the black entertainer in favor of the black inventor and new forms of collectivity.[172]

*

[172] However, one should remember the parodic dimension of Ra's alien drag and drag in general. While it is true that Ra might subvert the notion of explosive black masculinity, he still performs, from a feminist perspective, a very masculinized idea of leadership. From my point of view, one should take into account that I read Sun Ra's futurist alien as well as African despotic performativities as drag. Clearly underlining the performative dimension of race and the human, my point is precisely that Sun Ra subverts and parodies the notion of leadership instead of directly mimicking it. Even if he was radically seriously claiming that he came from Jupiter, one should not overlook the humorous dimension of his oeuvre.

7.0 The Arkestra: Sonic Ecstasy

*

I guess affect is the word I use for hope.

Brian Massumi[173]

Kara Keeling has already argued that the visual narrative in Blaxploitation has a special dialogue with the soundtrack. It comments on and complicates the experiences the hero has in the narrative and sometimes even adds another layer of critical discourse to the story. That music has a special place in black culture might have to do with the long exclusion of blacks from disciplines like writing and visual representation. This tendency is even further elaborated by the free jazz of the Arkestra, as it often, not always, breaks with conventional song structures and creates affective sounds that move towards the limit of what is considered music and melody. In *Space Is the Place*, music even possesses a stronger power than in other black films. Sometimes the sounds themselves produce interruptions in the story, thereby playing a notable part in producing black time-images, while in the scenes, the playing of the Arkestra itself is documented sonically and visually, which adds another time-image to the film beyond the narrative.

Already in the first scenes Ra comments that there is too much "sound of guns, anger, frustration" on Earth. Instead, Sun Ra's music signifies a different relation to the cosmos: sometimes in harmony with it and sometimes reflecting its multiple and creative chaos and complexity. This is also reflected by the cover art of his records, which were mostly produced by the Arkestra collectively. As Eshun has highlighted: "In

---

[173] Mary Zournazi and Brian Massumi, "Interview with Brian Massumi, Theorist, Montreal," *Assembly International: A Debate on Micro-Politics, Self-Organisation and International Affairs* (Berlin: b_books, 2005).

*

a strange way, your ears start to see."[174] Therefore the sounds of the Arkestra are the key to opening doors to new images, worlds, and temporalities. The live concert, and the Arkestra played a lot of them, therefore becomes the main ritual by which to leave the prison house of the present. The experimental, non-human, and affective nature of the live performance is extra-ordinary also in terms of its intensity, be it through the sheer volume of the noise produced by more than a dozen individuals that also affects the body of both band members and audience, or through the intense duration, as sometimes these concerts would go much beyond the usual convention of one to two hours. Thus, it produces a break with common subjectivities of the present and the everyday.

Interestingly, the final chapter of Muñoz's *Cruising Utopia* argues for a form of queer ecstasy, which should move people beyond a "here and now." The collective improvisatory and intensely affective practice of the Arktestra, which not surprisingly called one of its albums *Out There a Minute* (1989), can be seen as the perfect modus operandi for Muñoz's suggestion. He writes:

> We must vacate the here and now for a then and there. Individual transports are insufficient. We need to step out of the rigid conceptualization that is a straight present…. Willingly we let ourselves feel queerness's pull, knowing it as something else that we can feel, that we must feel. We must take ecstasy.[175]

174 Eshun 180.
175 Muñoz 185.

*

Obviously, Muñoz's statement that "we must take ecstasy" is not limited to its factual meaning. He translates the Greek term *ekstasis* as meaning "to be outside of oneself,"[176] which couldn't describe the effect of the Arkestra's practice better. While Muñoz refers to the music of the indie rock band The Magnetic Fields, it seems surprising that Sun Ra and his Arkestra are not even mentioned once in his book.

7.1 Collective Improvisation

> By placing all its components in continuous variation, music itself becomes a superlinear system, a rhizome instead of a tree, and enters the service of a virtual cosmic continuum of which even holes, silences, ruptures and breaks are a part.[177]
>
> Deleuze & Guattari

Far beyond the limited metaphors and sounds of The Magnetic Fields, jazz, especially free jazz with its deep relation to spontaneity, collective dialogue, and improvisation seems to deliver a whole world of sounds and melodies whose whole goal is to go beyond the everyday and create something new, at least on a micro-level. As the jazz composer Wynton Marsalis once said, jazz is based on the survival impulse of blacks in America through daily improvisation and also stimulates a permanent playing besides the normative sheet music. This existential dimension of jazz is also present through its affective level that hits the ear beyond normative effects of conventional songs and melodies. As Gilroy notes, music and performance in black

---

176 Muñoz 186.
177 Gilles Deleuze and Félix Guattari, *A Thousand Plateaus: Capitalism and Schizophrenia* (Minneapolis: University of Minnesota Press, 1987) 95.

*

cultures can't be explained mainly through textuality and narrativity, because the pre-discursive and anti-discursive components of black meta-communication happen on another affective level.[178] This level also transcends the boundaries between the bandleader, the group, and the audience. Thus, the whole space where the concert takes place is becoming cosmic music. As Jeremy Gilbert writes:

> In the impure spontaneity of real-time composition/performance there is necessarily a moment of becoming-music at which the boundaries between performer and performed, between audience and compositions, between music and instrument, between musicians and each other are all blurred: this is the moment of the opening onto 'the Cosmic' which is also an experience of sociality as such.... no element of music makes more vivid this dimension than the irreducibly social moment of improvisation.[179]

Clearly, the multiplicity and power of black sound are sometimes addressed by the lyrics of the Arkestra itself. As singer June Tyson sings in one of their few songs with lyrics: "The Sound of Joy is Enlightenment!" In this sense, the sound itself is supposed to have the power to enlighten the audience. Fascinatingly, the musicians of the Arkestra, who were sometimes known professionals, sometimes autodidacts, not only rehearsed a lot with their leader. Their music was also mainly inspired by his endless speeches about the politics of the cosmos and the potentiality of black subjectivity, as if his

---

178 Gilroy 75.
179 Jeremy Gilbert "Becoming-Music: The Rhizomatic Moment of Imrpovisation," *Deleuze and Music*, ed. Ian Buchanan and Marcel Swiboda (Edinburgh: Edinburgh University Press, 2004) 125.

*

teachings would translate directly into the music itself. Sometimes the music was even supposed to create a therapeutic power, as the 1967 album *Cosmic Tones for Mental Therapy* makes clear in its title. Gilbert also underscores the non-signifying dimension of collective improvisation:

> Collective improvisation always involves a non-signifying communication of energies, a complex dissemination of forces between the performers in an ensemble.... the sociality of improvising musicians is always constituted by transversal relations which cannot be understood in terms of any logic of signification.[180]

The practice of the Arkestra could be called endlessly processual. Permanent change of members, costumes, instruments, equipment, and lengths of the songs challenged the relationship between original and copy or interpretation, while the body of work the Arkestra accumulated might arguably be one of the biggest and most ambitious of modernity. As Sun Ra said himself, it doesn't matter if onstage or offstage, he and his band would always be rehearsing. Gilbert also notes that improvised music was often considered irrelevant in relation to the composed and structured genres of the west.[181] This narrative is considerably challenged by jazz, and especially free jazz of the Arkestra's kind. Gilbert also reminds us that all musics have an improvised dimension, but of course some do more than others. The ones with the most intense relation to improvisation would open up

---

180 Gilbert 124.
181 Gilbert 126.

*

the endless possibilities of sound itself.[182] This endless multiplicity was named "cosmic sound" by Deleuze and Guattari,[183] a term that literally was used by Sun Ra to describe his own music. For Ra, music was the most powerful language in the universe, as it would go beyond ethnicities and nations.[184] It is true that especially the abstract, noisy parts of the Arkestra's music makes it sound so non-human, so outer-worldly. Szwed remembers how "noise" was also directly associated with the music of the Arkestra as it gained its audience: "'Noise' was one of the first words which came to mind to many of those who heard Sun Ra's Arkestra in the 1960s. 'Noise,' in the abstract, is what scientists call phenomena which are unpredictable, out of control, beyond the system."[185]

Cover art: *Sun Ra & his Myth Science Arkestra* (1967)

182   Gilbert 135.
183   Deleuze and Guattari 379-381.
184   Szwed 120.
185   Szwed 228.

7.2 QuAre Assemblage Production

> To be an artisan and no longer an artist, creator, or founder, is the only way to become cosmic[186]
>
> Deleuze & Guattari

The practice of collective improvisation was central to the community of the Arkestra. Touring endlessly, being together all the time like in a spaceship, every single day rehearsing for many hours:

> ...they were like scientists... like Einstein. [They]'d rehearse all day and right up till you performed, get off at 4 a.m., rehearse at 12 until 4, then back again... The long rehearsals were part of his plan, a way of building up stamina and testing commitment. One of the musicians estimated that they practiced 180 hours for every hour that they played in public. It was not unusual for them to rehearse for hours before the gig, pack up their instruments, and proceed right to the performance.[187]

From a posthumanist perspective, instruments could also be seen as becoming prosthetics of the body, making the members look (and act) like musical cyborgs. But in the communal life of the Arkestra, which also provided a family for blacks with social problems or a past of addiction or prison, the production of costumes, performances, records, and cover art would also be part of daily life. If we look at the offensively white canon of queer art, one is tempted to call the collective work and life of the Arkestra a social factory, as Andy

---

186 Deleuze and Guattari 345.
187 Szwed 119.

*

Warhol's communal space of production was called. Like in Warhol's factory, life and art would blur and create a very unique and productive interface. Szwed emphasizes how open the Arkestra was to including new members at nearly any moment, coming from all walks of life:

> ...musicians from the very best music schools and amateurs; intellectuals and comedians; those who had given up otherwise lucrative careers and those who had never held a job; and sociopaths whom only their mothers, the army, or prison might be able to restrain.[188]

Sun Ra was able to make this collective machine work at an extraordinary level and succeeded in representing a collectivity in jazz that was slowly fading away. While the sixties were the time when jazz became more individualized as an industry and more and more musicians tried to make it through their own name and profile, and big bands often had to split because continuing them would have been too expensive, the Arkestra did hold a true counterposition to this trend, always symbolizing black collectivity, even in economically difficult times. At the same time, the quAre assemblage communal life of the Arkestra also posed an alternative to normative models of kinship and the nuclear family.

---

188 Szwed 116.

*

The quAre assemblage of the Arkestra, live in London, 2010

Deleuze and Guattari used the concept of the assemblage to describe collective transversal structures of interacting forces and subjects without a clear hierarchy. Assemblages are complex, non-dualistic networks and constellations, which go beyond the limited scope of subject positions. While subjects and identities are part of assemblages, they are named as a part among many other elements, including material forces and practices, technologies and objects, machines and prosthetics. Of course the musicians have identities, but these identities are not central and become more than their parts in the collective process. In a sense, the spaceship including all its elements is a good depiction of an assemblage. As the Deleuze Studies page of the Manchester Metropolitan University puts it:

*

> An assemblage is the dynamic interconnection of congruent singularities that remove the subject/object interface, yet retain elements of specificity. The human assemblage is a multiplicity that forms new assemblages with existing social and cultural assemblages of material movement, force and intensity.[189]

The quAre assemblage of the Arkestra not only becomes the metaphorical, but also the material space where new sounds and therefore new forms of blackness are invented and experimented with. Collective sound fuels this endless process and is always open to include new heterogeneous forms of black sound. Not surprisingly, Ra called his musicians "tone scientists."[190] Unlike the conventions of artistic profiling and soloist virtuosity, Ra claimed that in the Arkestra no played sound would be wrong per se. Either the collective was on the right track towards space or it was not: "The lesson was that it was a common enterprise and that solutions to the problem were a collective matter."[191] As John Corbett also argues about the best moments of jazz improvisation: "There is no longer a single player per se. In its place stands the figure of an assemblage..."[192] In a sense, the assemblage of the Arkestra was permanently invested in the endless process of inventing new forms of blackness itself. As Szwed comments on the special science, which could not be broken down to logics and models, that the Arkestra was inventing:

---

189 See: http://www.eri.mmu.ac.uk/deleuze/on-deleuze-key_concepts.php
190 Quoted in Eshun 161.
191 Szwed 114.
192 Corbett 84.

*

> For Sonny "science" was somewhere between or beyond science fiction and science. More than a method of reasoning and a set of laboratory practices, it was also a mystical process, and (as the rappers imply by "dropping science") a kind of secret or suppressed knowledge which had the power to create new myths, erase old ones, altering our ratio to each other and the rest of the universe. His thinking stemmed from an age when science, Hermetic philosophy, and magic were not so distinct, as well as from an earlier African-American understanding of "science" which meant a magic based on writing, and where science might include "conjure" or even "blackness" itself.[193]

In a radical sense, the assemblage of the Arkestra was permanently invested in the endless process of inventing new forms of blackness itself. In the words of Eshun, it assembled counter-mythologies, permanently mixing "science and myth and vice versa."[194] This was especially clear by the inventive way that Ra used the Moog synthesizer, which becomes an affective, amplifying field intensifying the multiple, affective connections with both the band and the audience. As Eshun elaborates:

> He's turning the Moog synthesizer into something like a circuit which can act as a giant alternating current between the people listening, the Arkestra and the cosmos itself. The Moog is the amplifier that directs currents in and out.... So you get this idea of music as this sonic production circuit through which — as Gilles Deleuze was saying — molecules of new people may be

---

193 Szwed 132.
194 Eshun 158.

planted here or there. That's very much what Sun Ra's doing: he's using the Moog to produce a new sonic people…. He's using it to produce the new astro-black American of the '70s.[195]

As if the universe were playing piano — and inventing Blackness anew: Cover art from Sun Ra: *Monorails and Satellites* (1967)

*

195 Eshun 184-185.

8.0 Outro

*

In this book I have tried to look at the paradigm of post/slavery as an important epistemological break within predominately white gender and queer studies and how motifs of black locality, mobility, and temporality can be used productively for a specifically quAre perspective. After trying to grasp the trauma and passivity of the loop of colonial time in Fanon, I looked at the cinema classic of *Birth of a Nation* to demonstrate how images of the black as the sexualized monster and the *black danger* (moving through public space) have survived in post-slavery times. This sexualization of racism has been a central factor in exclusivist ideologies and has been reappropriated and turned around, as I argue, in the first emancipatory black cinema, Blaxploitation. Following the circulation of the media images of the armed Black Panthers, this cinema, which I also try to categorize as a minoritarian cinema and a black movement-image, reappropriated images of the *explosive* black and the *sexual* black for its own purposes. Through an intersectional perspective I also tried to show that this cinema progressed considerably over time, providing space for more and more complex main characters and representational constellations, including black revolutionary women (with guns) and also queer subtexts.

Through a discussion of black queer perspectives I try to understand these films as quAre. As I showed, from a quAre perspective it is not the main distinction of hetero and homosexuality that shapes quAre subject formations, but more complex intersections of whiteness and blackness, gender, sexuality, and a classically white, nationalist notion of heteronormativity that shapes the ones excluded by it, such as "punks, bulldaggers, and welfare queens," but also avant-garde composer and performer Sun Ra and the members of his social factory

*

and commune, the Arkestra. With Muñoz's notions of queer utopia I tried to open the perspective of a quAre futurity that understands queerness as a critical position against a totalizing present and for a quAre future of hope and fabulation. This perspective I linked with the discourses of Afrofuturism and the black diaspora, two discourses that not only provide a useful backdrop to understand the practice and politics of Sun Ra and his Arkestra, but also show an alternative to limited discourses of black nationalism and violent struggle. Furthermore, Afrofuturism and the black diaspora create an echo of the disturbing images and deeds of slavery itself, while twisting its trajectories for emancipatory purposes. In this sense, the slaveship becomes the spaceship, and the Middle Passage the Black Atlantic, now multi-layered spaces of multitemporal articulations that both remember slavery and open up to forms of progress between Africa and the Americas.

In my final analysis I looked at Sun Ra's visual and sonic politics, most notably in my analysis of John Coney's 1974 film *Space Is the Place*. This film marks a distinction between the black movement-images of Blaxploitation and the complex time-images that are included in its own construction. Ra's quAre and cosmic intervention also asks us to look differently at black common sense and its heroes, especially the black macho who became the main protagonist of Blaxploitation and through its black authenticity the common sense image of black liberation. In my final analysis of the main practice of the Arkestra, the concert in its noisy and performative form, including collective improvisation and alien drag, I turn to Deleuze again to grasp the non-signifiying practices of free jazz interaction as well as the communal and non-familiaristic way of living and producing together as

*

one quAre assemblage. This assemblage not only questions narrow framings of the human and presentist intersectional approaches that solely concentrate on marked identity-profiles instead of looking at their practices and alternative visions, but at the same time uses the extraordinary example of Sun Ra to gesture towards a canon of quAre articulations that are not founded on the continuation of a (unconsciously or not, but nevertheless) white universalist narrative. Radically quAre, the perspective of Sun Ra asks for nothing less than a black universalism, in which the phenomenon of blackness itself is the object of continuing reconsideration and invention. This critical but affirmative position might inspire us to a new approach to quAre politics, which for too long has been treated as a marginal issue. The interaction with this issue, for both me, the writer, and you the reader, is not just proposed as a strategical intervention into some sort of canon, but as a way of remembering past crimes which cannot be erased, and pursuing future utopias that not only might change the canon of white queer studies, but also the political imaginary of anybody motivated to critique sexism, racism, homophobia, and nationalism alike. However, every end of a book is only a stop at another intersection, another constructed ending. There is always more to be learned and more to be understood in regards to racism or sexism, especially by a white, male author. As white Jewish-American philosopher Avital Ronell reminds us on the impossibility of a finished result — or meaning at all in a limited vulgar sense of the word in regards to the other:

If we're not anxious, if we're okay with things, then we're not trying to explore or figure anything out. Anxiety is the mood par excellence of ethicity... This is something that Derrida has taught: If you feel that you've acquitted yourself honorably, then you're not so ethical. If you have a good conscience, then you're kind of worthless.... The responsible being is one who thinks they've never been responsible enough, they've never taken care enough of the Other. The Other is so in excess of anything you can understand or grasp or reduce... You can't presume to know or grasp the Other. The minute you think you know the Other, you're ready to kill them.... If you don't know, if you don't understand this alterity — that it's so Other that you can't violate it with your sense of understanding — then you have to let it live in a sense.[196]

*

---

[196] Quoted from *Examined Life*, dir. Astra Taylor, 2008.

9.0 Bibliography

(online resources last viewed on December 15, 2012)

Andrews, William L., and Henry Louis Gates Jr., eds. *Slave Narratives*. New York: The Library of America, 2001.

Aloni, Udi, with Slavoj Zizek, Alain Badiou, and Judith Butler. *What Does a Jew Want? On Binationalism and other Specters*. New York: Columbia University Press, 2011.

Althusser, Louis. "Ideology and Ideological State Apparatuses," *Lenin and Philosophy*. New York: Monthly Review Press, 1971.

Attali, Jacques. *Noise: The Political Economy of Music*. Minneapolis: University of Minnesota Press, 2009.

Bhabha, Homi. "What does the Black Man Want?" *New Formations, Remembering Fanon*, No. 1, Spring 1987.

Bignall, Simone, and Paul Patton, eds. *Deleuze and the Postcolonial*. Edinburgh: Edinburgh University Press, 2010.

Bloch, Ernst. *The Principle of Hope*, Vol. 1. Cambridge: MIT Press, 1986.

Bowles, Nathaniel Earl. *My Music is Words: The Poetics of Sun Ra*. Thesis submitted to the faculty of the Virginia Polytechnic Institute and State University, 2008. Link: http://www.scribd.com/doc/24713038/My-Music-is-Words-%E2%80%93-the-Poetics-of- Sun-Ra

Broecks, Susanne. "Das Subjekt der Aufklärung – Sklaverei – Gender Studies: Zu einer notwendigen Relektüre der Moderne," *Gender Kontrovers – Genealogien und Grenzen einer Katgorie*, ed. Gabriele Dietze and Sabine Hark. Köngistein/Taunus: Ulrike Helmer Verlag, 2006, 152-180.

Buchanan, Ian, and Marcel Swiboda, eds. *Deleuze and Music*. Edinburgh: Edinburgh University Press, 2004.

Buck-Morrs, Susan. *Hegel, Haiti, and Universal History*. Pittsburgh: University of Pittsburgh Press, 2009.

Butler, Judith. "Endangered Endangering – Schematic Racism and White Paranoia," *The Judith Butler Reader*, ed. Sara Salih with Judith Butler. Malden/Oxford: Blackwell Publishing, 2004, 204-212.

Campbell, Robert M. *From Sunny Blound to Sun Ra: The Birmingham and Chicago Years*, 2011. See http://hubcap.clemson.edu/~campber/sunra.html

Carson, Clayborne. *Zeiten des Kampfes. Das Student Nonviolent Coordinating Commitee (SNCC) und das Erwachen des afro-amerikanischen Widerstands in den sechziger Jahren*. Nettersheim: Verlag, 2004.

Cervulle, Maxime. "Erotic / Exotic. Race and Class in French Gay 'Ethnic' Pornography," *Post / Porn / Politics*, ed. Tim Stüttgen. Berlin: b_books, 2010, 180-189.

Casarino, Cesare. *Modernity at Sea: Melville, Marx, Conrad in Crisis*. Minneapolis: University of Minnesota Press, 2002.

Castronovo, Nelson, ed. *Materializing Democracy: Toward a Revitalized Cultural Politics*. Durham: Duke University Press, 2002.

Corbett, John. *Extended Play: Sounding Off from John Cage to Dr. Funkenstein*. Durham: Duke University Press, 1994.

Corbett, John, Anthony Elms, and Terri Kapsalis. *Pathways to Unknown Worlds: Sun Ra, El Saturn and Chicago's Afro-Futurist Underground 1954-1968*. Chicago: White Walls, 2006.

Costa, Sergio. *Vom Nordatlantik zum Black Atlantic*. Bielefeld: Transcript Verlag, 2007.

Crenshaw, Kimberle. "Demarginalizing the Intersection of Politics and Sex: A Black Feminist Critique of Antidiscrimination Doctrine, Feminist Theory and Antiracist Politics," *The University of Chicago Legal Forum Volume: Theory, Practice and Criticism*. Chicago: University of Chicago Press, 1989.

Delany, Samuel R. *Trouble on Triton: An Ambigous Heterotopia*. Middletown: Wesleyan Universiy Press, 1976.

Davis, Angela. *Women, Race and Class*. London: The Women's Press, 1983.

Deleuze, Gilles. *Cinema I: The Movement-Image*. London: Athlone Press, 1986.

Deleuze, Gilles. *Cinema II: The Time-Image*. London: Athlone Press, 1989.

Deleuze, Gilles, and Félix Guattari. *A Thousand Plateaus: Capitalism and Schizophrenia*. Minneapolis: University of Minnesota Press, 1987.

Dery, Mark, ed. Flame Wars: *The Discourse of Cyberculture*. Durham: Duke University Press, 1994.

Diederichsen, Diedrich, ed. *Loving the Alien: Science Fiction, Diaspora, Multikultur*. Berlin, ID Verlag: 1998.

Dietze, Gabriele, and Sabine Hark, Sabine. *Gender Kontrovers – Genealogien und Grenzen einer Kategorie*. Königstein/Taunus: Ulrike Helmer Verlag, 2006.

Dorestal, Philipp. *Style Politics: Mode, Geschlecht und Schwarzsein in den USA, 1943-1975*. Bielefeld: Transcript Verlag, 2012.

Du Bois, W.E.B. *The Souls of Black Folk*. Mineola: Dover Publications, 1994.

Edelman, Lee. *No Future: Queer Theory and the Death Drive*. Durham: Duke University Press, 2004.

El-Tayeb, Fatima. *European Others – Queering Ethnicity in Postnational Europe*. Minneapolis: University of Minnesota Press, 2011.

Eshun, Kodwo. *More Brilliant Than The Sun: Adventures in Sonic Fiction*. London: Quartet Books, 1998.

Fanon, Frantz. *The Wretched of the Earth*. New York: Grove Press, 2004.

Fanon, Frantz. *Black Skin, White Masks*. New York: Grove Press, 2008.

Ferguson, Roderick A. *Aberrations in Black: Towards a Queer of Color Critique*. Minneapolis: University of Minnesota Press, 2004.

Foucault, Michel. "Of Other Spaces," *Diacritics* No. 16, 1986.

Foucault, Michel. *Society Must Be Defended: Lectures at the Collège de France, 1975-1976*, ed. Mauro Bertani and Alessandro Fontana. New York: Picador, 2003.

Freeman, Elizabeth. *Time Binds: Queer Temporalities, Queer Histories.* Durham: Duke University Press, 2010.

Gilroy, Paul. *The Black Atlantic: Modernity and Double Consciousness.* Camdridge: Harvard University Press, 1993.

Gilroy, Paul. *Darker than Blue: On the Moral Economies of Black Atlantic Culture.* Cambridge: Belknap Press of Harvard University Press, 2011.

Gilroy, Paul, Tina Campt, and Haus der Kulturen der Welt, eds. *Der Black Atlantic.* Berlin: Haus der Kulturen der Welt / Vice Versa, 2004.

Gill, John. *Queer Noises: Male and Female Homosexuality in Twentieth-Century Music.* Minneapolis: University of Minnesota Press, 1995.

Gramsci, Anotinio. *Selections from the Prison Notebooks.* New York: International Publishers, 1971.

Grier, Pam. "Es Geht Nur Um Körper. Interview mit M. Stocker," *Süddeutsche Zeitung*, 19 Aug. 2006. http://www.sueddeutsche.de/kultur/385/306347/text/.

Halberstam, Judith. *In a Queer Time and Place.* New York: New York University Press, 2005.

Haraway, Donna. *Simians, Cyborgs and Women: The Reinvention of Nature.* New York: Routledge, 1991.

Hartman, Saidiya V. *Scenes of Subjection: Terror, Slavery, and Self-Making in Nineteenth-Century America.* Oxford: Oxford University Press, 1997.

Heble, Ajay. *Landing on the Wrong Note: Jazz, Dissonance and Critical Practice.* New York: Routledge, 2000.

Hill, John, and Pamela Church Gibson, eds. *The Oxford Guide to Film Studies.* Oxford: Oxford University Press, 1998.

Johnson, E. Patrick. *Appropriating Blackness: Performance and the Politics of Authenticity.* Durham: Duke University Press, 2003.

Johnson, E. Patrick, and Henderson, Mae G., eds. *Black Queer Studies.* Durham: Duke University Press, 2005.

Keeling, Kara. *The Witch's Flight: The Cinematic, the Black Femme, and the*

Image of Common-Sense. Durham: Duke University Press, 2007.

Kerner, Ina. *Differenzen der Macht. Zur Anatomie von Rassismus und Sexismus*. Frankfurt am Main: Campus Verlag, 2009.

Kreis, Daniel. "Appropriating the Master's Tools: Sun Ra, the Black Panthers, and Black Consciousness, 1952-1973," *Black Music Research Journal*, Vol. 28, No.1, Spring 2008.

Kracauer, Siegfried. *From Caligari to Hitler: A Psychological History of the German Film*. New York: Princeton University Press, 1947.

Lock, Graham. *Blutopia: Visions of the Future and Revisions of the Past in the Work of Sun Ra, Duke Ellington, and Anthony Braxton*. Durham: Duke University Press. 1999.

Martin-Jones, David, ed. *Deleuze and World Cinemas*. London: Continuum, 2011.

McBride, Dwight A. *Why I Hate Abercrombie & Fitch: Essays on Race and Sexuality*. New York: New York University Press, 2005.

Mc Call, Leslie. "The Complexity of Intersectionality," *Signs: Journal of Women in Culture and Society*, Vol, 30, No. 3, 2005.

Mercer, Kobena. *Welcome to the Jungle: New Positions in Black Cultural Studies*. New York: Routledge, 1994.

Muñoz, José Esteban. *Disidentifications: Queers of Color and the Performance of Politics*. Minneapolis: University of Minnesota Press, 1999.

Muñoz, José Esteban. *Cruising Utopia: The Then and There of Queer Futurity*. New York: New York University Press, 2009.

Nnaemeka, Obioma. "Bodies That Don't Matter: Black Bodies and the European Gaze," *Mythen, Masken und Subjekte. Kritische Weißseinsforschung in Deutschland*, ed. Eggers et al. Münster: Unrast Verlag, 2005.

Niganni, Chrysanthi and Merl Storr, eds. *Deleuze and Queer Theory*. Edinburgh: Edinburgh University Press, 2009.

Pelligrini, Anne. *Performance Anxieties: Staging Psychoanalysis, Staging Race*.

New York: Routledge, 1991.

Puar, Jasbir K. *Terrorist Assemblages: Homonationalism in Queer Times.* Durham: Duke University Press, 2007.

Puar, Jasbir K. "Ich wäre lieber ein Cyborg als eine Göttin. Intersektionalität, Assemblage und Affektpolitik." European Institute for progressive Cultural Policies, 2011. Link: http://eipcp.net/transversal/0811/puar/de

Reid-Pharr, Robert. *Once You Go Black: Desire, Choice and the Black American Intellectual.* New York: New York University Press, 2007.

Rollefson, J. Griffith. "The 'Robot Voodoo Power' Thesis: Afrofuturism and Anti-Anti-Essentialism from Sun Ra to Kool Keith," *Black Music Research Journal*, Vol. 28, No. 1, Spring 2008.

Sarreiter, Bene. *Black Dynamite*, 2011. See: http://www.arte.tv/de/2860746,CmC=2861278.html

Siegel, Marc. "Jack Smith Glauben Schenken," *Golden Years: Materialien und Positionen zu queerer Subkultur und Avantgarde zwischen 1959 und 1974*, ed. Diederichsen et al. Vienna: Camera Austria, 2008.

Somerville, Siobhan B. *Queering the Color Line: Race and the Invention of Homosexuality in American Culture.* Durham: Duke University Press, 2000.

Spillers, Hortense. "Mama's Baby, Papa's Maybe: An American Grammar Book," *Diacritics*, Vol. 17, No. 2, Summer 1987.

Spivak, Gayatri Chakravorty. "Can the Subaltern Speak?" *Marxism and the Interpretation of Culture*, ed. Cary Nelson & Lawrence Grossberg. Chicago: University of Illinois Press, 1988, 297.

Stoler, Laura-Ann. *Race and the Education of Desire: Foucault's History of Sexuality and the Colonial Order of Things.* Durham: Duke University Press, 1995.

Stüttgen, Tim, ed. *Post / Porn / Politics.* Berlin: b_books, 2010.

Stüttgen, Tim and Jasbir K. Puar. "Ein Knotenpunkt von vielen. Interview mit der Queer-Theoretikerin Jasbir K. Puar zu Fragen des Posthumanismus,"

Vienna: *Springerin*, 1/13, 2013.

Szwed, John. *Space Is the Place: The Life and Times of Sun Ra*. New York: Payback Pressm, 1997.

Tinsley, Omise'eke, Natasha. (2008): "Black Atlantic, Queer Atlantic: Queer Imaginings of the Middle Passage," *GLQ: A Journal of Lesbian and Gay Studies* 14.2-3, 2008.

Toop, David. *Haunted Weather: Music, Silence and Memory*. London: Serpent's Tail, 2004.

Verevis, Constantine. "Minoritarian & Cinema," *The Deleuze Dictionary*, ed. Adrian Parr. Edinburgh: Edingurgh University Press, 2010, 165-167.

Wallace, Michelle. *Black Macho and the Myth of the Superwoman*. London: Verso, 1990.

Wilmer, Val. *Obituary: Sun Ra. The Independent*. London, 1. July 1993. http://www.independent.co.uk/news/people/obituary-sun-ra-1482175.html

Wolter, Udo. *Das obscure Subjekt der Begierde. Frantz Fanon und die Fallstricke des Subjects der Befreiung*. Münster: Unrast Verlag, 2001.

Zournazi, Mary and Brian Massumi. "Interview with Brian Massumi, Theorist, Montreal," *Assembly International: A Debate on Micro-Politics, Self-Organisation and International Affairs*. Berlin: b_books, 2005.

Links of Imagery

(last viewed on December 15, 2012)

Saartje Bartman / Hottentot Venus. Found at: http://wahidahfowler.net/wp-content/uploads/2010/11/sarak_batman_venus_hottentot.jpg

"Black Mama White Mama." Theatrical poster. Found at: http://en.wikipedia.org/wiki/Black_Mama,_White_Mama

"Black Belt Jones" found at: http://en.wikipedia.org/wiki/File:Black_belt_jones_

movie_poster.jpg

"Brother From Another Planet." Theatrical poster. found at: http://en.wikipedia.org/wiki/The_Brother_from_Another_Planet

Dr. Octagon: "Dr. Octagonecologyst". Cover artwork found at: http://www.hhv.de/shop/de/artikel/dr-octagon-dr-octagonecologyst-72766

"Foxy Brown." Theatrical poster found at: http://www.imdb.com/title/tt0071517/

George Clinton & Parliament. "Mothership Connection." Cover artwork found at: http://www.geo- translations.de/LOUNGE/music5.html

Interview with Sun Ra conducted by Jennifer Rycenga. http://www.plonsey.com/beanbenders/SUNRA-interview.html

Janelle Monae. "Metropolis" and "Arch Android." Cover artworks found at: http://www.interpreten-m.musikverrueckt.de/html/janelle_monae_-_metropolis.html and http://www.culturebully.com/janelle-monae-archandroid-album-review

Map of the "Middle Passage" found at: http://www.waywelivednc.com/maps/historical/middle-passage.gif

Kool Keith: "Black Elvis/Lost in Space." Cover artwork found at: http://www.6pack.ch/catalog/product_info.php?products_id=7571

Mapplethorpe, Robert: "Cock and Gun" (1982). Photograph found at: http://www.nyphotoreview.com/NYPR_REVS/NYPR_REV1217.html

Lee "Scratch" Perry & Ari Up: "Welcome to Planet Dub." Cover-artwork found at: http://mp3.soundquake.com/shopserver/ActionServlet?sessionid=-sqs&cmd=albumdetails&labelid=1116591068846&albumid=1240574822962

"Black Panthers with Guns." Found at: http://xroads.virginia.edu/~UG01/barillari/pantherchap1.html

"Space Is the Place." Film still found at: http://colourschool.co.uk/category/music/

"Space Is the Place." Film still found at: http://photonmontage.blogspot.

177

com/2010/02/sun-ras-space-is-place.html

"Space Is the Place." Film still. Found at: http://thisisnothingnew.files. wordpress.com/2010/06/vlcsnap-3161694.png

"Space Is the Place." Film still. Found at: http://www.metamute.org/files/images/sunra_communitycentre.preview.jpg

"Space Is the Place." 2 Film stills. Found at http://ryfigueroa.blogspot. com/2010/12/sun-ra-missing-link-between-duke.html

"Sweetback's Bad Badass Song." Theatrical poster. Found at: http://www. electricsheepmagazine.co.uk/reviews/wp- content/uploads/2007/05/review_ sweetback.jpg

Sun Ra's Arkestra (live in London). Found at: http://www.pcah.us/blog/entry/a-conversation-with-the-sun-ra-arkestra/

Sun Ra & his Solar Myth-Arkestra. "Cosmic Tones for Mental Therapy" (1967). Cover-Artwork. Found at: http://en.wikipedia.org/wiki/Cosmic_Tones_for_Mental_Therapy

Sun Ra: "Monorails and Satellites" (1968). Cover artwork. Found at: http:// en.wikipedia.org/wiki/Monorails_and_Satellites

Sun Ra: Portrait. Found at: http://www.lastfm.de/music/Sun+Ra/+images/22624369

Sun Ra on Detroit TV, 1981. USA 1981. http://www.dangerousminds.net/comments/sun_ra_on_detroit_tv_1981/

Sun Ra, the Berkeley Lectures, USA 1971. http://www.eastofborneo.org/archives/sun-ra-the-berkeley-lectures-1971

Sun Ra: Space Is the Place. Cover artwork. Found at: http://elrataz.blogspot. com/2008/08/sun-ra-space-in-place.html

Sun Ra and his Solar Arkestra Visit Planet Earth, Cover artwork. Found at: http://en.wikipedia.org/wiki/Sun_Ra_and_his_Solar_Arkestra_Visits_Planet_Earth

Films

Baadasssss! Marion van Peebles, 2003.

Baadasssss Cinema: A Bold Look at '70s Blaxploitation Cinema. Isaac Julien, 2002.

The Birth of a Nation. D.W. Griffith, 1915.

Black Mama, White Mama. Eddie Romero, 1973.

The Brother from Another Planet. John Sayles, 1984.

Cleopatra Jones. Jack Starret, 1973.

Coffy. Jack Hill, 1973.

Examined Life. Astra Taylor, 2008.

Fort Apache, The Bronx. Daniel Petrie, 1981.

Foxy Brown. Jack Hill, 1974.

Germania, anno zero [Germany Year Zero]. Roberto Rosselini, 1948.

Gone with the Wind. Victor Fleming, 1939.

Jazz. Ken Burns, 2000.

A Joyful Noise. Robert Mugge, 1980.

The Last Angel of History. John Akomfrah, 1997.

Roots. TV-miniseries, various directors, 1977.

Queen. TV-miniseries, John Erman, 1993.

Space Is the Place. John Coney, 1974.

Sun Ra: Brother from Another Planet. Don Letts, 2005.

Sweet Sweetback's Bad Badasssss Song. Melvin van Peebles, 1974.

Acknowledgements by the Author

Tim Stüttgen would like to thank: the b_books collective, Liad Kantorowicz, Max Jorge Hinderer, Margarita Tsomou, Katya Sander, Carsten Juhl & the Fine Art Academy of Copenhagen for great support and creative realization of this book, Eveline Kilian and Elahe Haschemi Yekani for fruitful feedback and supervision in an earlier version of this text, Aloxsia Tudor and Gökçe Yurdakul for making me learn more about intersectionality at my studies at HU Berlin.

The Author

Tim Stüttgen a.k.a Timi Mei Monigatti, born 1977 in Solingen Germany,† Mai 12.2013 in Berlin. Tim was a philosopher, writer, performer, curator, member of b_books, a great friend and the hardest working queen on the post porn scene. Besides countless live performances all over the world, he was also part of the cinematic post porn poem: *Arrêt la machine! postpone postporn happiness* (PAF/mimosa productions 2007). He studied film studies, fine art, and gender-queer theories in London (Middlesex University), Hamburg (Hochschule für Bildende Künste HH), Maastricht (Jan van Eyck Academie), and Berlin (Humboldt-Universität). His research covered issues such as the history of pornography and post-pornography, performance art, the visual histories of black liberation and post-slavery, sexwork, Michel Foucault, and Gilles Deleuze/Félix Guattari. As curator and activist, he has organized conferences, and festivals like *Post/Porn/Politics* (2006, Volksbühne, Berlin), *Genderpop!* (2008, Goethe-Institut, Athens), and *What's Queer About Queer Pop?* (2010, Hebbel-Am-Ufer, Berlin). In 2012 he co-initiated the collective theater play *Wir sind ein Bild aus der Zukunft* (Hebbel-Am-Ufer, Berlin). Tim wrote for various international political and cultural magazines and published as editor volumes such as *Post Porn Politics – The Symposium Reader* (2009, b_books, Berlin).

Post-Sciptum: Editors' notes

The Department of Language, Space & Scale at the Royal Danish Academy of Fine Arts has long been dedicated to discussions of contemporary art's relation to issues of power, space, and architecture, as they are informed by feminism, post-colonial studies, and queer theory.

As part of our ongoing questioning of identity, body, race, sexuality, desire, and gender, we invited Tim Stüttgen to Copenhagen to lead a seminar with the point of departure in his paradigmatic book *Post/Porn/Politics*. In the fall of 2011 he arrived at the academy, not only with an explosion of energy, but also bringing with him entire universes of examples and practices: people, texts, images, films, links, music, and much more. When he left, we had all had our minds blown. Through his fast thinking, extensive research, and tireless accumulation and re-configuration of material, he led us on endless journeys, always curious, always searching for new routes. We were especially impressed by the way in which he let his academic life and art practices interweave, fuse and inform each other, always searching, always experimenting, always pushing, speculating, trying; always letting life and thought merge, without limits.

Stüttgen's practice not only as an academic, but also as a radically experimenting performer, filmmaker, imageproducer, and collaborator, was a brilliant example of how and why artistic research is so vital: relentlessly probing, finding, getting involved with, and thinking through material, as well as constantly testing, re-organizing, and realizing his own responses to it. He was committed to never respecting disciplinary borders; not those set up by academia, nor those set up by art, but only to finding out more and learning more — always along with others, be it colleagues, collaborators, participants, spectators, or students. His practice emphasizes the enormous potential of this kind of research: creating unexpected connections that re-inscribe unacknowledged parts of knowledge production back into bodily experience.

This was why we invited Stüttgen to write a book in the framework of the artistic research program of the Academy.

When he returned to the department a year later — the fall of 2012 — to lead his next seminar, he thus brought with him the manuscript for *IN A QU*A*RE TIME AND PLACE* together with an overwhelming amount of material: images, music, films, texts, anecdotes, ideas, etc. We had talked about the possibility of opening up his process of researching and writing the book for the students without compromising the integrity of his work, and Tim generously decided simply to bring the chapters and go through them, one every day, discussing with the students the questions he tried to ask, the material he used, and the ways in which he navigated forward through it. It became a very intense seminar where Tim did not simply demonstrate to the students how he worked, but rather involved them directly as colleagues and equals; discussing his drafts and doubts, going through his examples and following routes to conclusions, taking note of the questions, critiques and confusion they expressed, and also re-working parts of his arguments accordingly. His radical openness and demand for unfiltered critique and engaged, collective thinking left them deeply inspired, infused, infiltrated. Tim Stüttgen's input has made a seminal mark in our study-program, and it was with great sadness that we learned about his death. Though he hadn't finalized his manuscript, his work will continue to resonate, and it is with great pride that we can now publish his book. We are thankful to b_books and the people close to Tim who have put such extraordinary work into bringing his writing the last step to the stage of publishing, and we know, in the spirit of Tim, that the work is never over, never done, it will always be infinitely unfinished.

Katya Sander
Professor, Department of Language, Space & Scale
The Royal Danish Academy of Fine Arts

*

On editing the last manuscript post mortem

As editors of this book, we were in the privileged but difficult position of editing the text after Tim Stüttgen's untimely death. Almost every decision that was necessary for the final manuscript was a difficult one, and even seemingly simple questions took on a heavy weight since we were forced to answer for Tim. In this text, we would like to clarify what we did (and did not do) with the final manuscript that Tim Stüttgen left us.

The manuscript was in its final stage, complete with everything necessary before going to print: bibliography, full footnotes, and acknowledgments. Thus it was much more a finished manuscript than a posthumous fragment, and our job was merely to look over language issues and check spelling and punctuation details. Though Tim was not a native English speaker, he was very comfortable speaking and writing in English, and there were very few serious language problems to be corrected in the text. We made the decision early on not to 'correct' his occasionally untypical phrasing and style so as not to strip the text of its particularity, its voice, and its charm.

The only major change made to the text has to do with the extensive use of italics. In the final manuscript, Tim had adopted a somewhat complex system of italicization, which he explains in Chapter 01.01. In addition to the standard use of italics, he italicized words referring to (constructed) categories of power, terms of category, and derogatory terms. In his owns words, they were meant to "produce a sensibility for the categories of power and relational categories in question and make the reader, in a sense, stumble again and again over the italics and thereby become sensitive to the relational categories s/he is dealing with."

While this can be read as an intriguing method for dealing with the malices of language, at the same time it raised a wide number of inconsistencies. Each of Tim's categories is far from fixed, so it was unclear where to draw the line, for instance between constructed and non-constructed. A further question was whether the difficulty of reading the text was in fact a positive 'stumbling,' or merely a difficulty.

We entered into a lengthy discussion about whether or not to follow the system as it is given in the final manuscript. Even as we go to press, the discussion has not died down, partly because both decisions seem wrong to us. Some are of the opinion that it would have been better to leave the manuscript as the author left it, especially because he explained his method in his foreword; others think it was appropriate to change it, knowing that Tim himself was undecided as to whether to keep the italics of not. In the end it was decided not to follow the author's system and to "straighten out" the terms in italics. While we consider both options as valid, and both indeed as correct had Tim chosen them, they both seemed wrong when the decision was left to us. No matter what choice we made, we felt like we were betraying Tim. For that reason, we would here like to give a brief impression of what is now no longer visible in the published text.

The italics were numerous on every page and created a strong visual impression of movement and energy, resisting the dominant power of language and continually reminding the reader of its arbitrary quality. The italicization practice seemed like a deliberate gesture to refuse easy legibility, but also like a courageous act of fighting with a language that Tim always tried to bend in his work as both journalist and author. He often used visual markers like stars, underlining, slashes, etc. and invented new words in his writing. To give some specific examples, he italicized the classic constructed categories such as race, gender, sexuality, class and their relatedness with adjectives like white/black/queer/quAre, but also male/female, homosexual/heterosexual. The second type of italics were political concepts that followed the categories of power like queer feminism, white gaze, black authenticity, gender difference, black sexuality, black science fiction, and the third were negative and derogatory terms that he tried to call into question by italicizing them like explosive, phallic, or homophobic black man, black danger, black animal/white human, etc. This list of terms conveys how urgently Tim wanted to point out the subtle violence of language between class, race, and gender, but also gives an indication of the problem: that this method of italicization cannot ever really be self-contained and has a tendency to frazzle out at the margins. The italics are thus symptomatic of the way Tim was dealing with being an intellectual — trying to exceed given concepts, not respecting and going beyond limits of academia or journalistic rules, which can both enrich or endanger a text.

In the published text here, the italics have more or less been restricted to standard English usage, although we couldn't resist leaving in one or two of Tim's special cases. We hope the reader doesn't mind.

Daniel Hendrickson, Margarita Tsomou
Berlin, October 6, 2014

*